Inventory
adamo-faiden

Inventory: Record of goods and other things belonging to a person or a community, made with order and precision. (Dictionary of the Royal Spanish Academy).

This book is built from images, drawings and texts. These three types of documents are exposed in an elemental way, alone in the center of each page and isolated from the project to which they belong. We organized our inventory from a set of documents that first claim their independence and then undergo a peer dialogue. These two actions may seem to cancel each other out, but they actually both reaffirm a very basic idea, which holds that the interest of a conversation is closely related to the consistency of its interlocutors. The conversation that arises from each diptych is precisely what stimulates the appearance of a tacit project. A project that bypasses material organizations and that is only possible due the intervention of an active reader, capable of establishing connections between the documents printed here. Because this is an inventory that calls for participation. It requires an inquisitive gaze, eager to move from the beginning to the end and back to the beginning, over and over again, finding unexpected connections, potential projects or ideas. Paradoxically, this wide range of interpretation is possible thanks to the simplicity of its structure: a systematic accumulation of diptychs that builds a linear and intentional journey. This carefully designed tour covers a great diversity of scales crystallized in five types of associations, which, interspersed with written essays, end up defining each point of view.

In summary, this book seeks to respond to the two mottos raised in the definition of “inventory”. What are the disciplinary assets that our architecture studio produces? How should we organize them to accurately delineate our interests?

Lago houses

33 Orientales 138 building

33 Orientales 138 building

Bonpland 2169 building

Arribeños 3182 building

Ático Boulevard Labrador building

Oro 1778 parking

11 de Septiembre 3260 building

Puertos mixed-use complex

Gonzalo Ramírez 1441 social housing

La vecindad Plaza Mafalda building

La vecindad Plaza Mafalda building

La vecindad Plaza Mafalda building

Conesa 4560 building

Martos house

Bedaberes house extension

Martos house

Bedaberes house extension

Andes 1143 social housing

Andes 1143 social housing

Venturini house

La Cándida community center

Di Tella University pavilion

33 Orientales 138 extension

Deseos

Mid-week house

Sáenz house

Cepé house

Cepé house

Puertos sports club

Chalú house

Puertos mixed-use complex

Sociedad del Mar summer residences

Figueroa house

La Juanita's shed

Miraflores house

Catalinas square

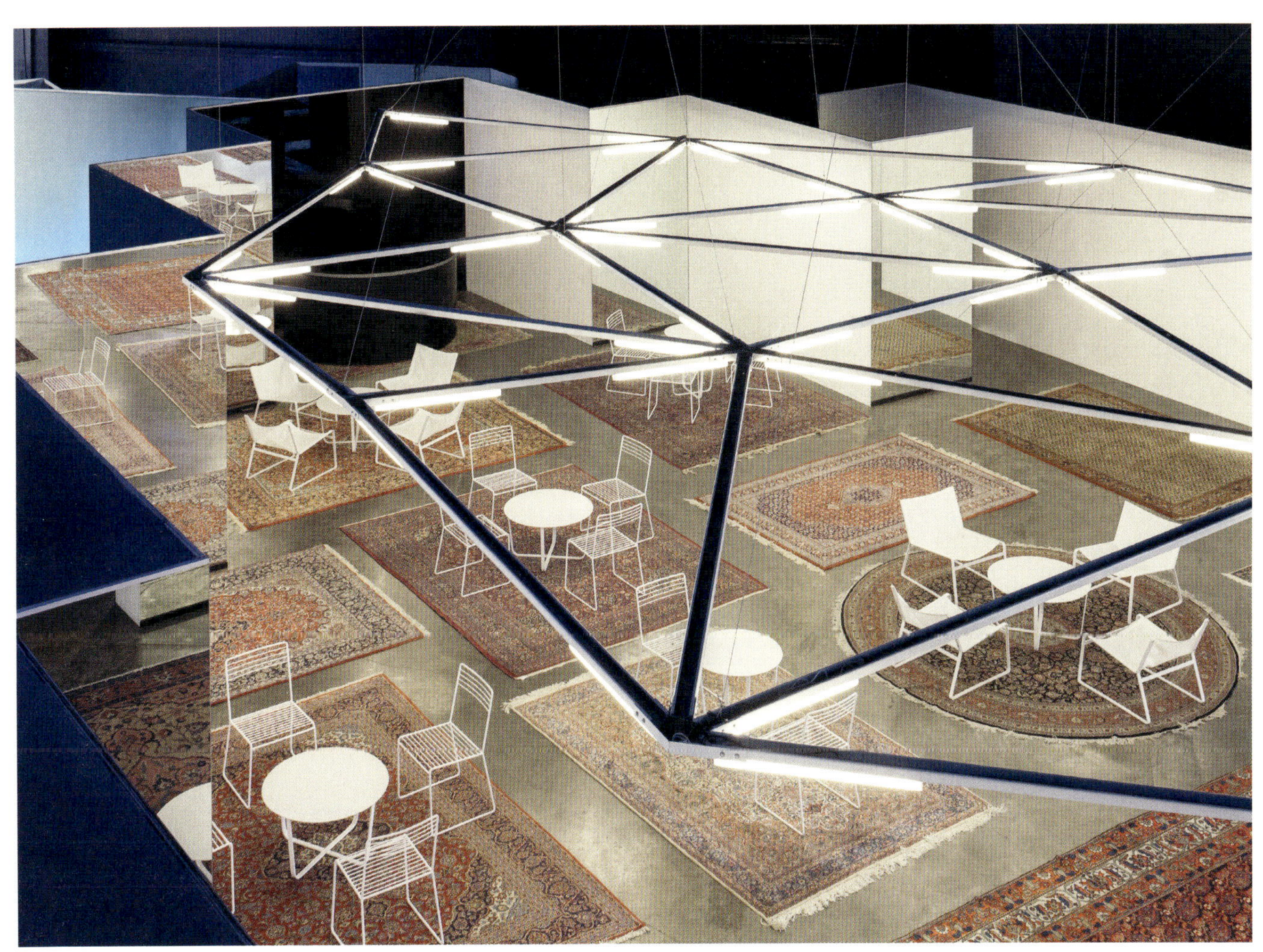

VIP room arteBA

Gianelli mixed-use complex

Huergo 475 tower

O'Higgins 1625 building

O'Higgins 1625 building

MuReRe Project

The MuReRe Project (mutualism, residential, regenerative) promotes a form of non-expansive growth of urban land. In contrast to the social and programmatic homogeneity with which Latin American cities increase their footprint, we promote a scenario in which the overlapping of uses and coexistence groups can redefine the meaning of any infrastructural framework that demands more energy than it provides. The detection of this imbalance will force us to readjust the equations that structure each landscape, thus serving as the jumping off point for the project. From there, we will formalize a new contract between housing and environment. Like in biological mutualism – where both species seek to improve their skills by interacting with one another – we will interact hand-in-hand with the pre-existing architecture. We will abandon the empty plot or virgin land to find the necessary support for typological innovation on those rooftops that have the potential to expand.

In this sense, our task will go beyond the technical and material world to enter the social relations that this process will unleash. Giving shape to the desires and needs of the inhabitants of both strata will require the construction of new design techniques capable of synthesizing the complexity of each episode.

Our objective, then, will no longer be the alignment of cornices or stylistic continuity and will focus instead on the production of the necessary effects that anticipate a deep and radical development. That is why we will refer to a *mestizo* urbanism, much more tactical than strategic, with the capacity to regenerate the urban fabric over very short periods of time. To that end, we will act as mediators, intermediaries or diplomatic agents of worlds that will no longer seem disconnected from us. The construction of new relationships will be the main object of the MuReRe Project.

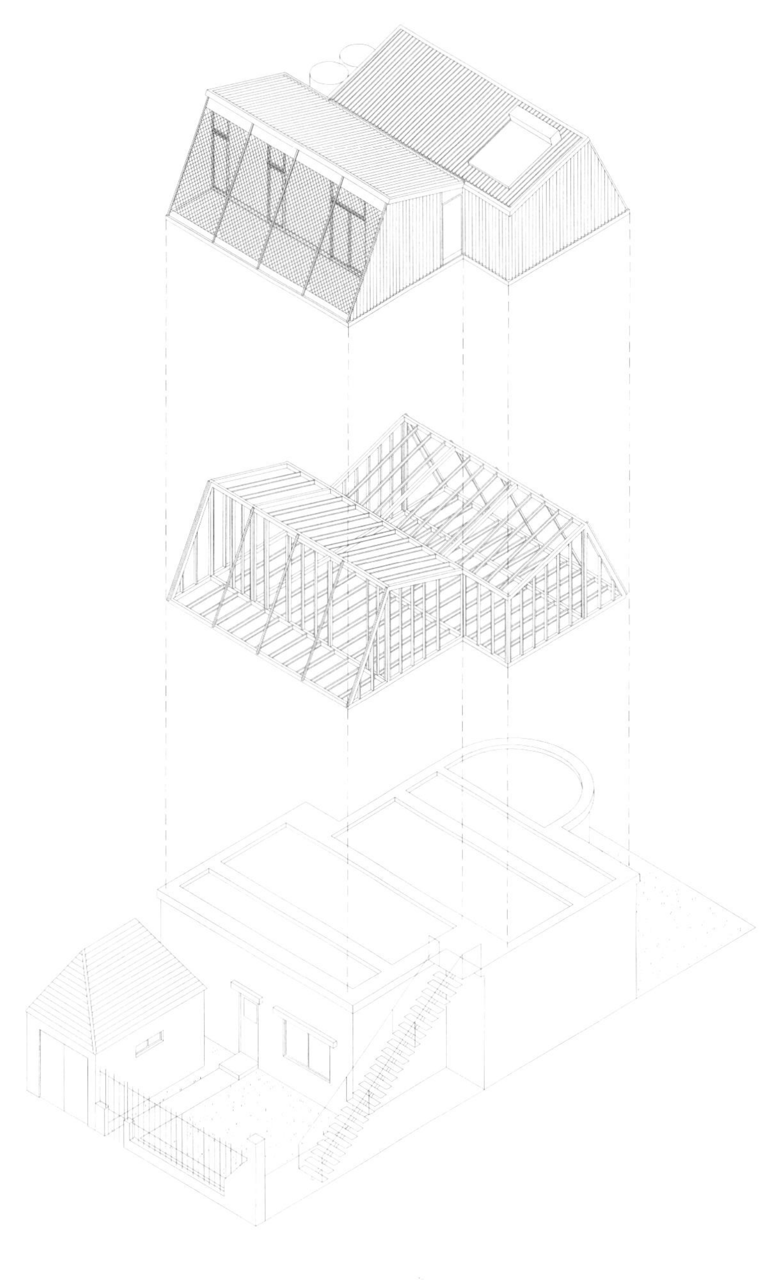

MuReRe houses

MuReRe houses

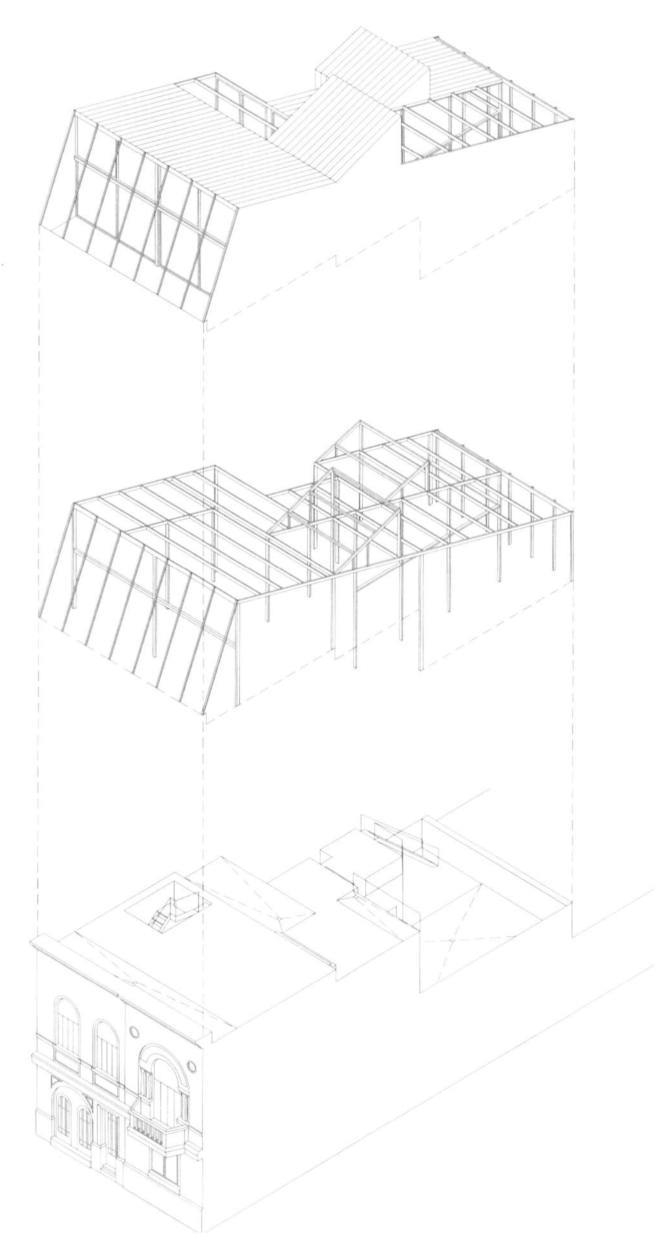

Blas house extension

Blas house extension

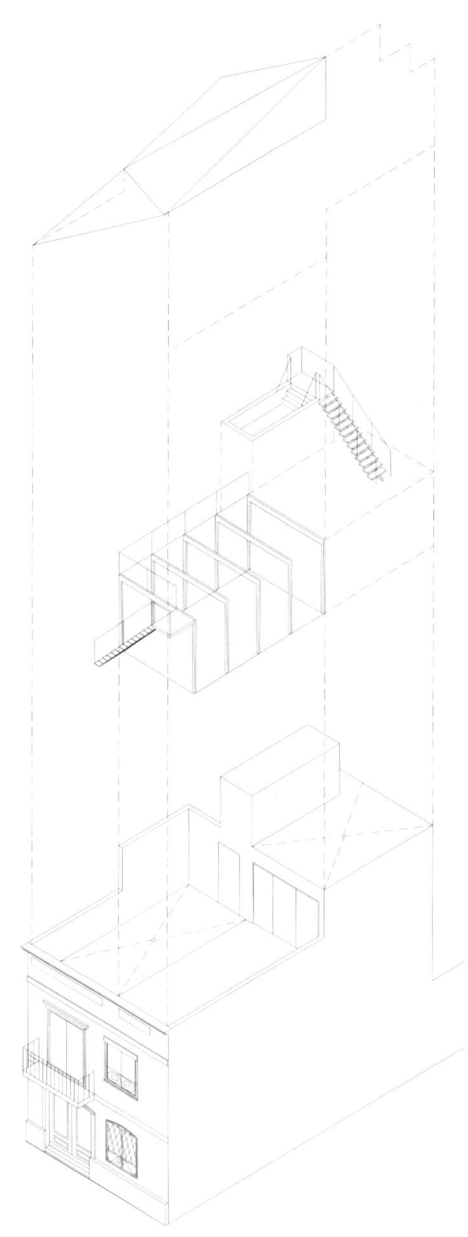

Núñez house extension

Núñez house extension

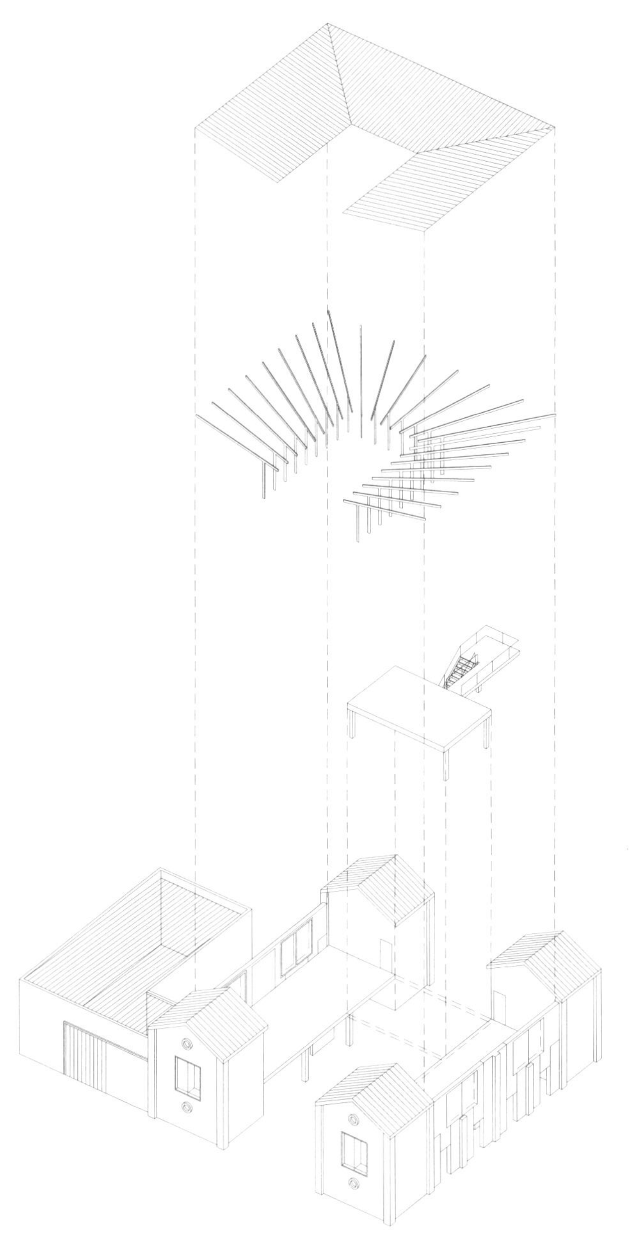

Macchi house extension

Macchi house extension

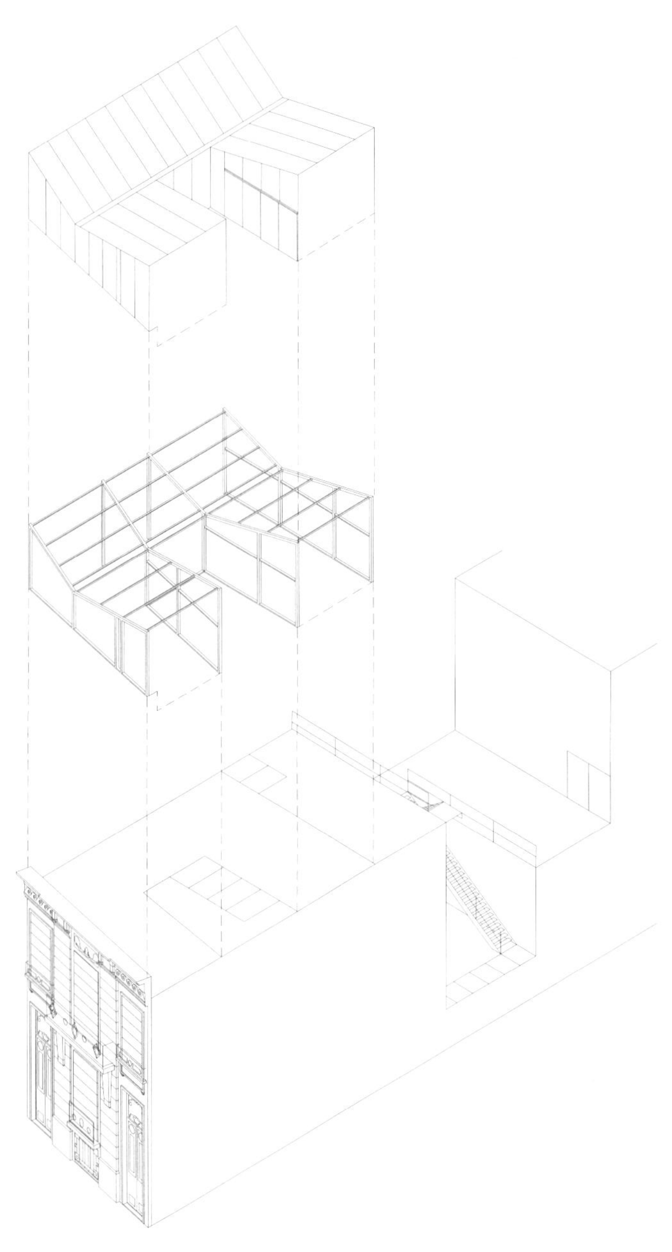

Venturini house extension

Venturini house extension

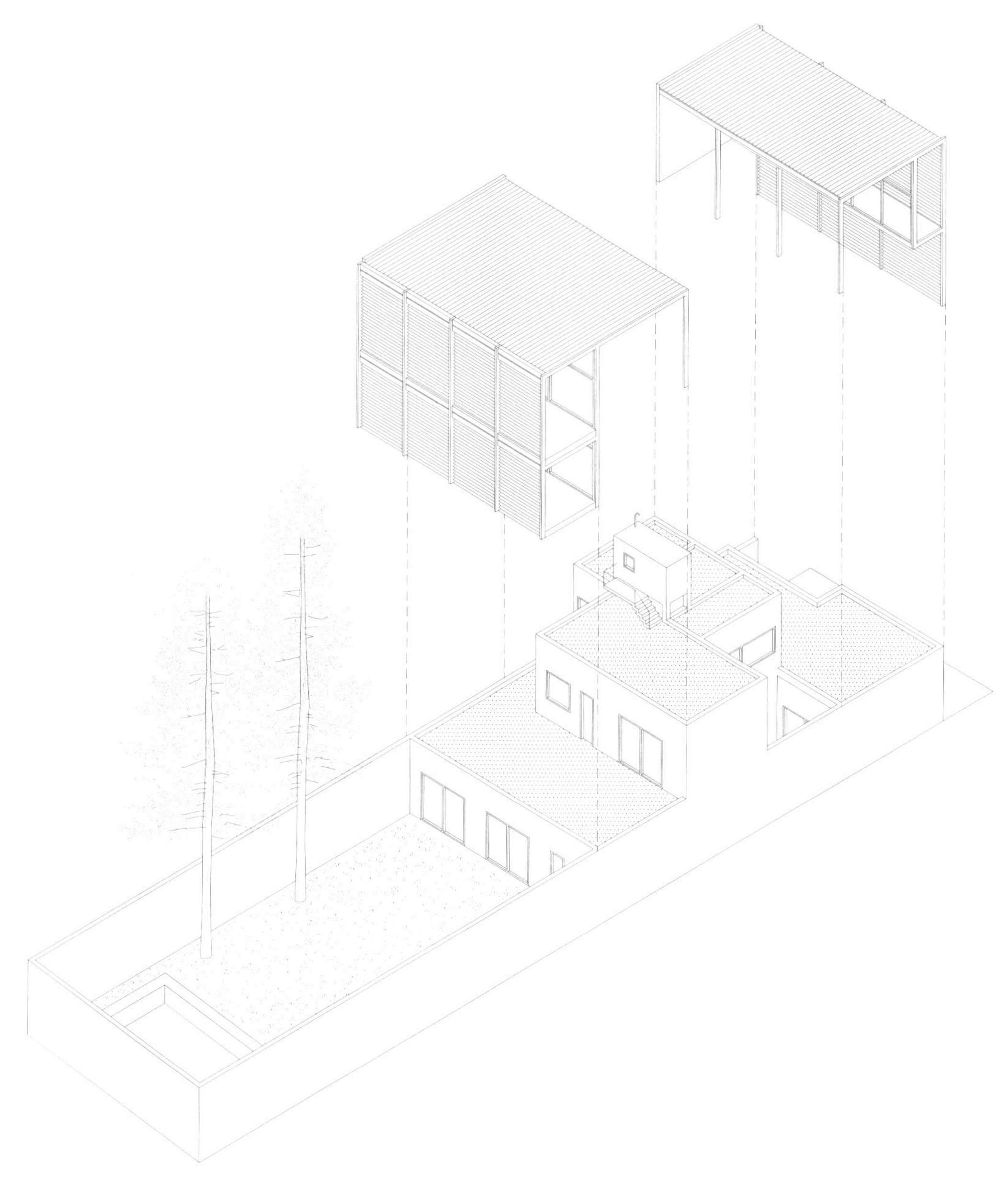

Bernardello house extension

Bernardello house extension

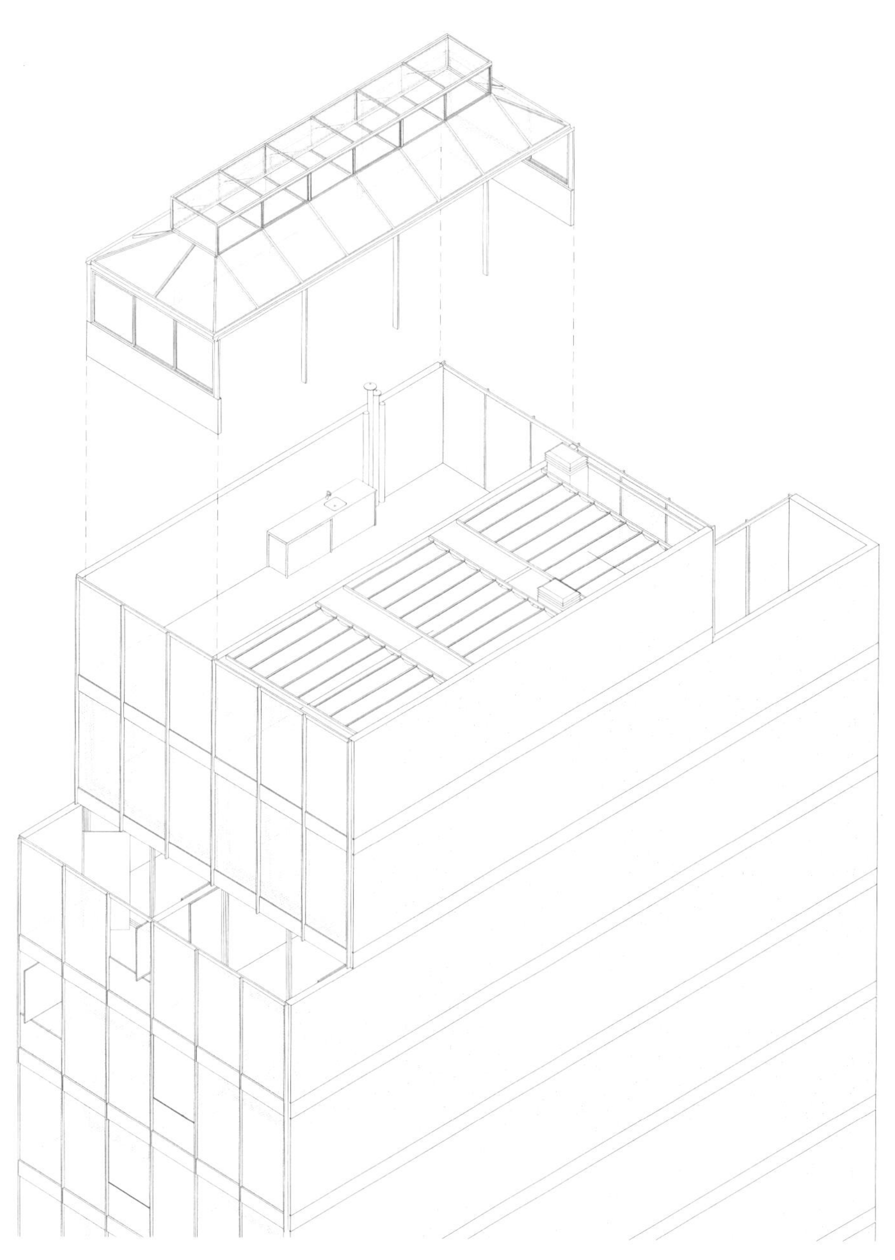

33 Orientales 138 extension

33 Orientales 138 extension

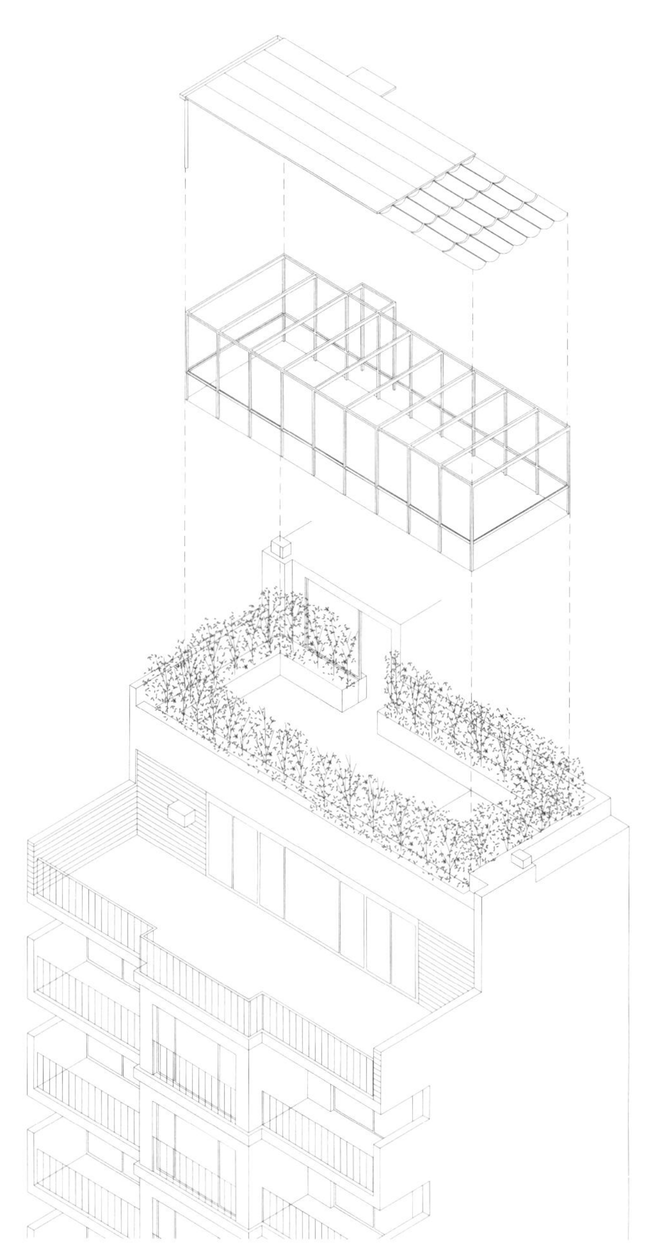

Piñeiro house extension

Piñeiro house extension

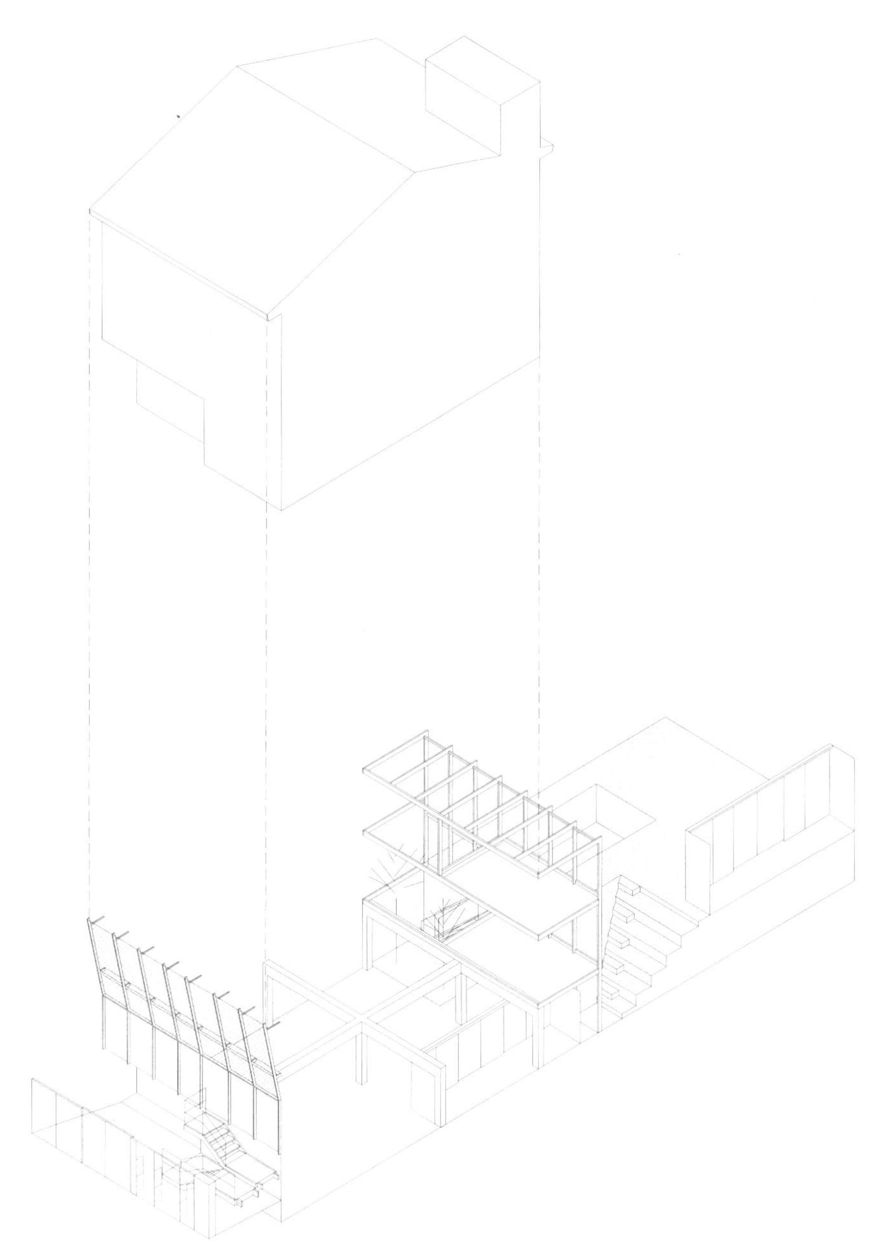

Fernández house extension

Fernández house extension

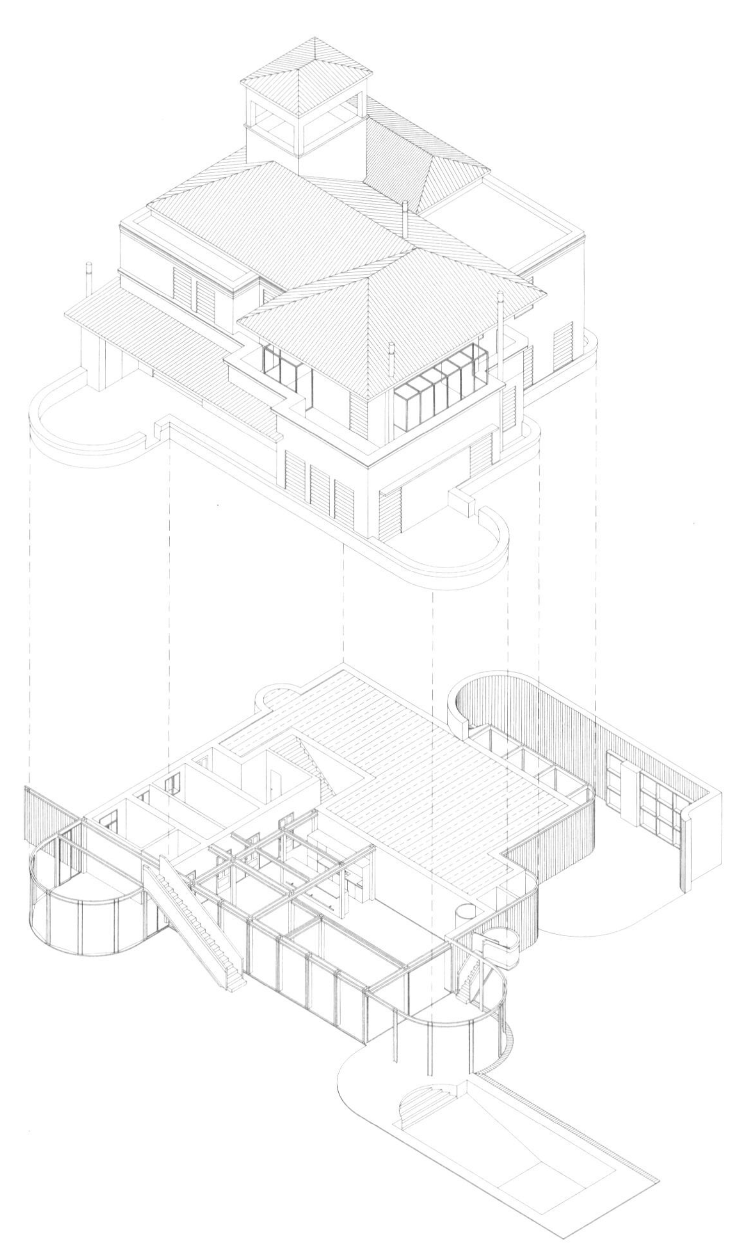

Luar house extension

Luar house extension

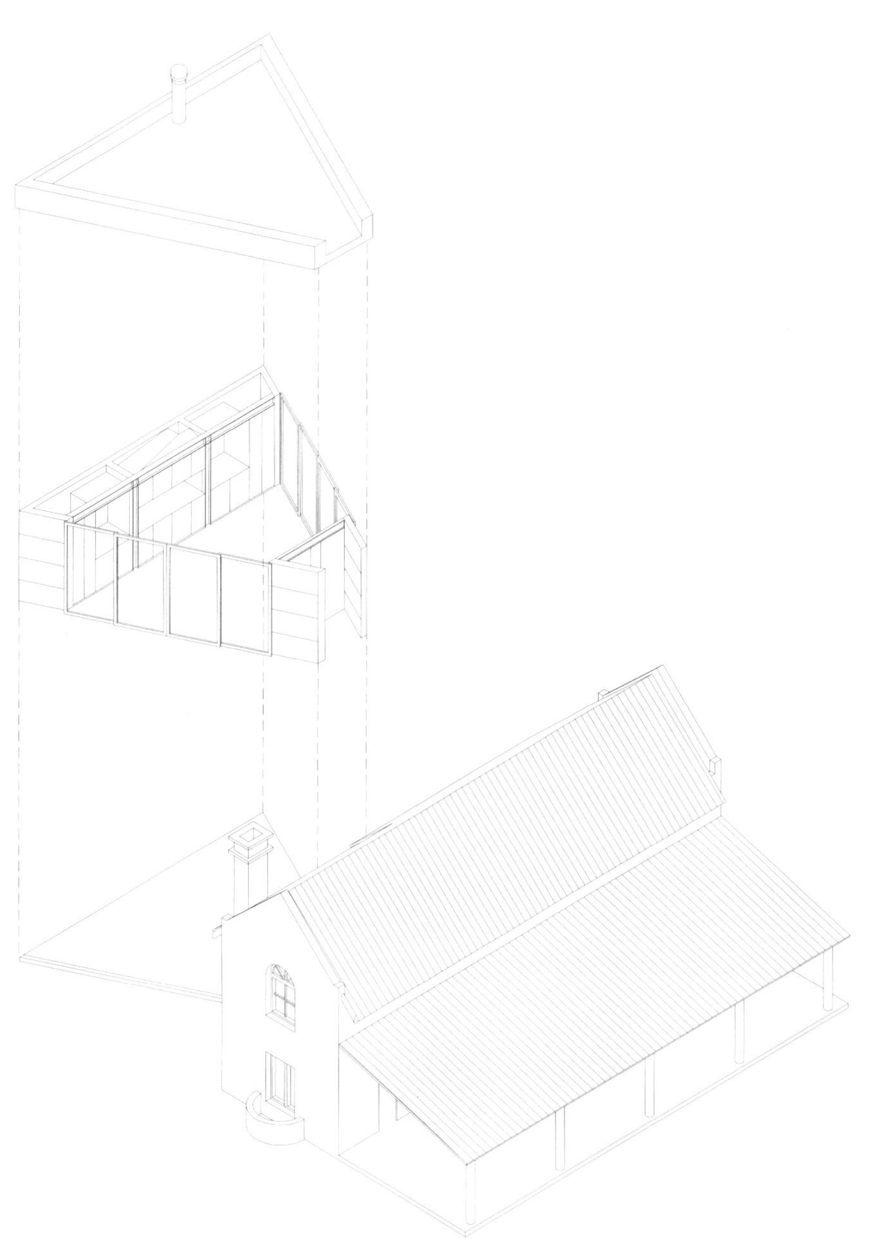

Salgado house extension

Salgado house extension

Optical retail

CRYSTALVISION
optica

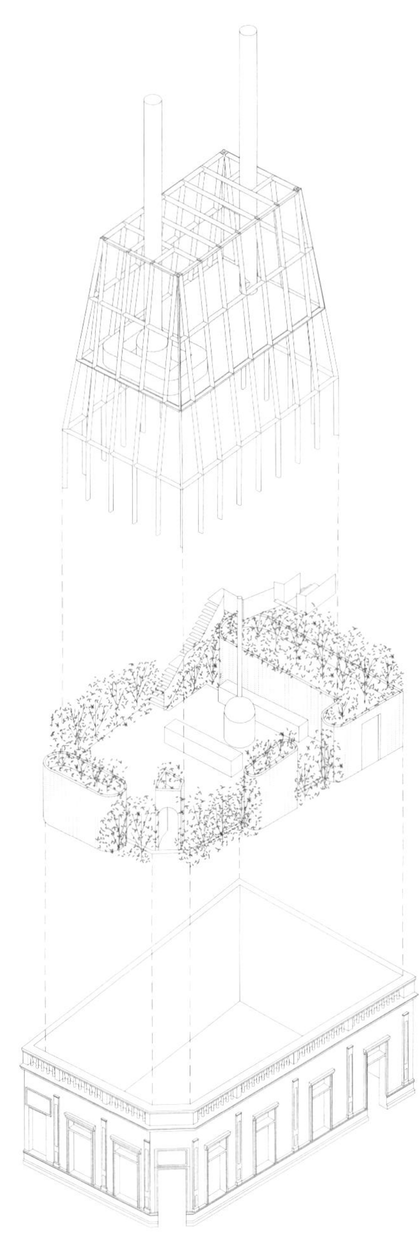

Orno pizzeria

Orno pizzeria

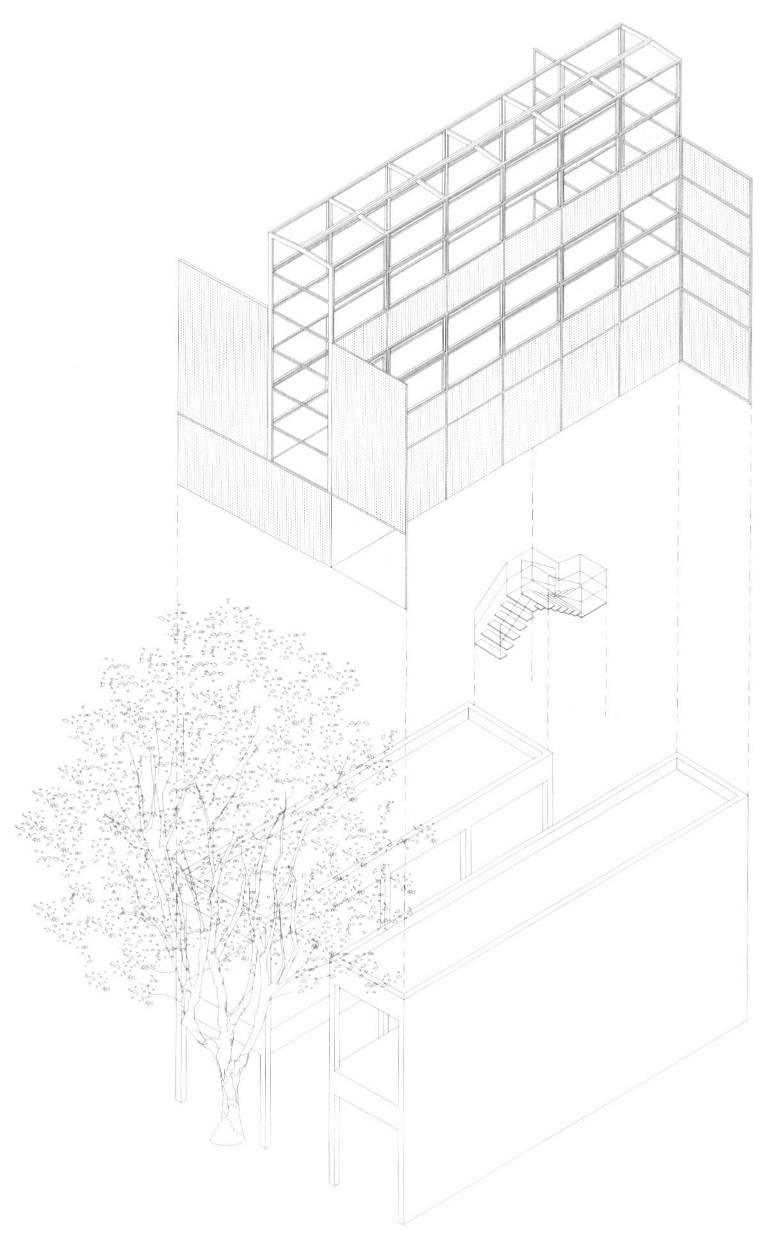

Guayaquil 650 veterinary clinic

Guayaquil 650 veterinary clinic

A Permeable Curtain Wall

Architecture is a form of knowledge. We have thousands of years of accumulated experiences that, over time, have been distilled into an inexhaustible catalog of design techniques. Even so, every new project presents its own variables, preventing us from reproducing the same decisions that others have already made. This gap between disciplinary knowledge and contingency is what drives our practice. It is what allows us to have a historical projection and to be attentive to our day to day. The result of this attitude produces architectures that are familiar to us while projecting their own agenda – without nostalgia, but also without a fascination for novelty. We are interested in working where we find room for ambiguity, positioning ourselves in the cracks of the established categories to procure a greater margin of action, of freedom.

Designing an intermediate climate is an action plan that ties in with those ideas. Focusing on a specific place, but with a close relationship to the external weather and the internal standards of comfort. Built both with natural soil and plant species, as well as with light and industrialized materials, these are instances which we cannot call gardens or rooms. In all cases, they are deregulated spaces that seek to transfer the same freedom to the inhabitants that we want for our practice.

By overlapping with the climate of Buenos Aires, the modern curtain wall radically changes its configuration. Pushed by the strong rains and solar radiation, the glass recedes from the outer edge of the façade. This displacement creates an intermediate space that can be used to build raised gardens in tune with the city's huge trees. The exterior surface of this new curtain wall no longer has to solve the watertightness of the building but rather support its vegetation, resolve solar control or, on some occasions, act as a filter capable of mediating the building's security. These new demands have an impact on the materiality of the enclosures. Their perception becomes more permeable than that of their predecessors, allowing them to reveal all their physical and ideological depths. Paradoxically, the formal and constructive continuity they present is a stimulus for their renewed expressiveness.

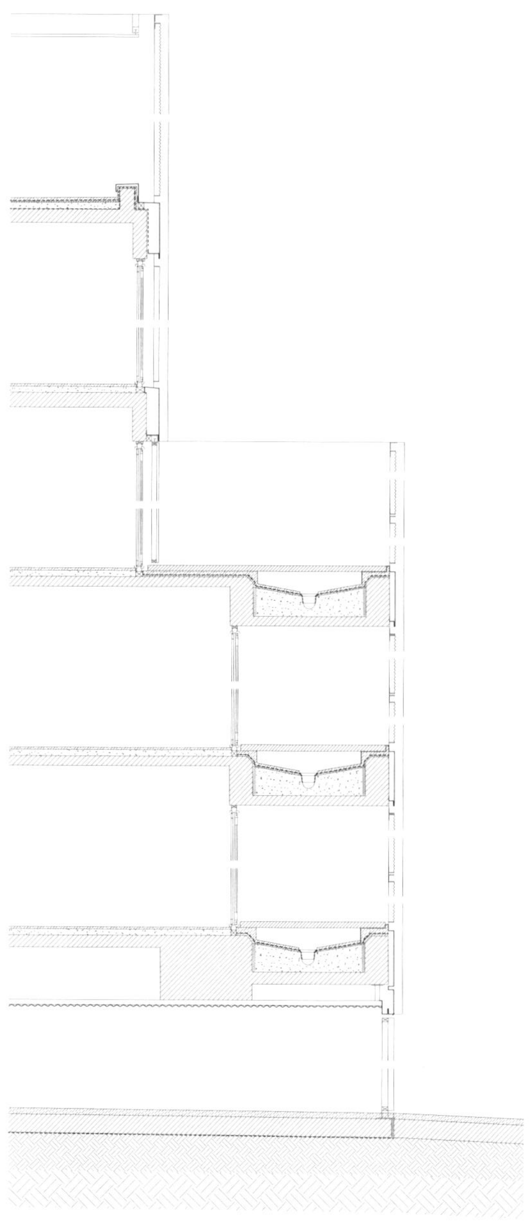

33 Orientales 138 building

33 Orientales 138 building

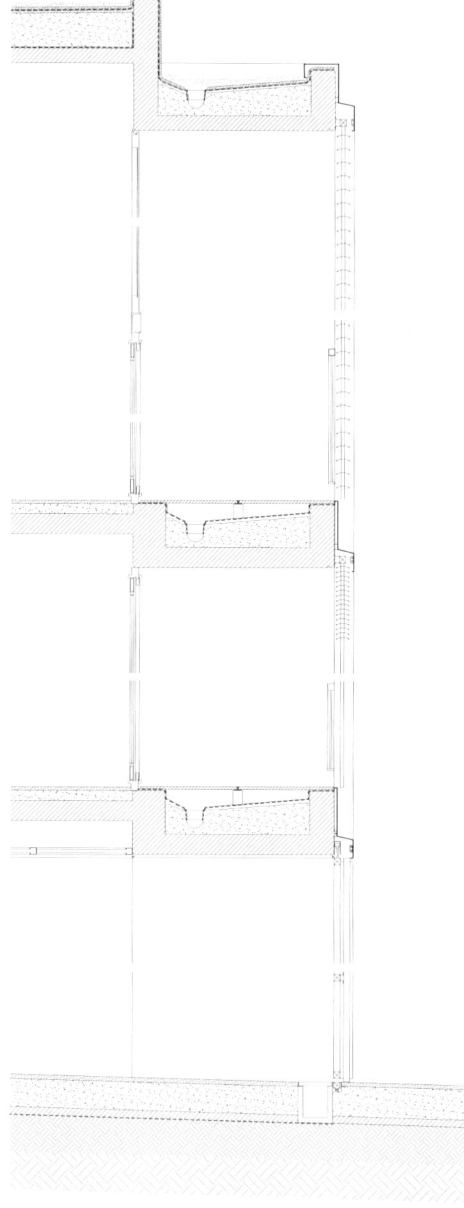

Arribeños 3182 building

Arribeños 3182 building

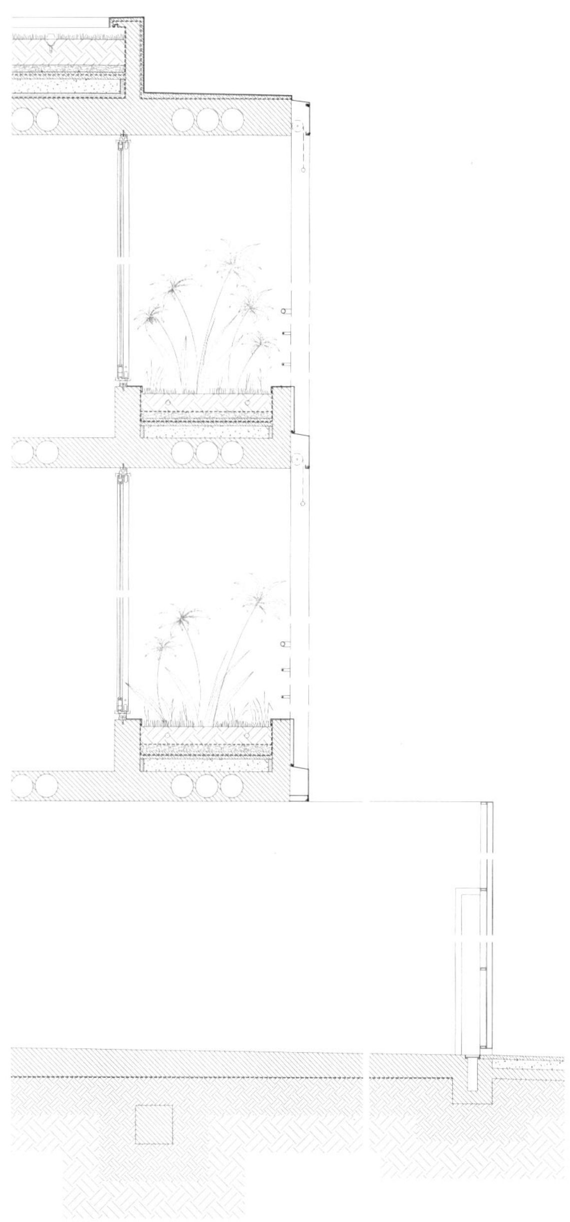

11 de Septiembre 3260 building

11 de Septiembre 3260 building

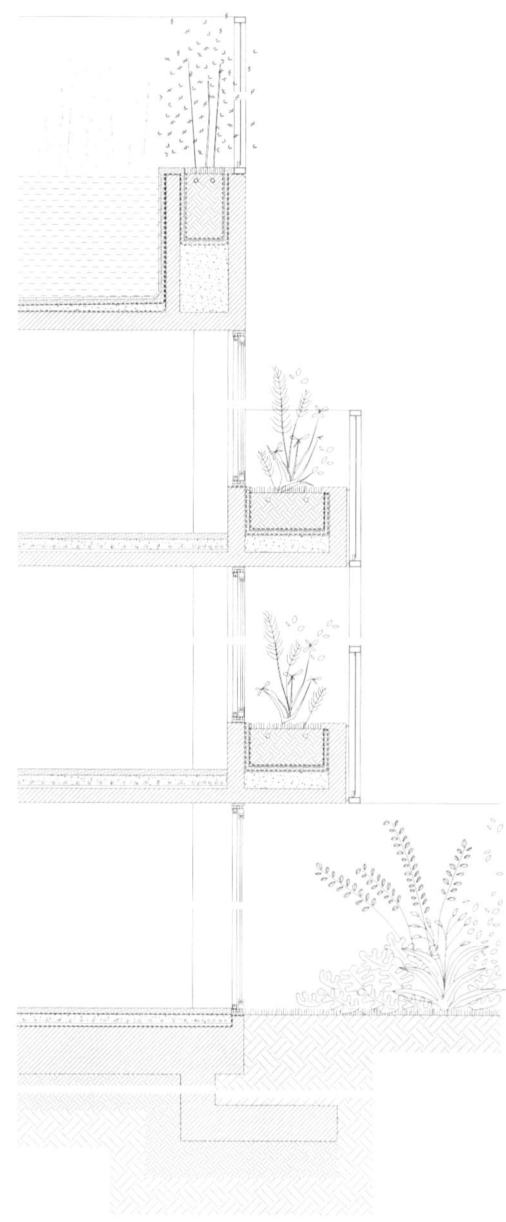

Bedaberes house extension

Bedaberes house extension

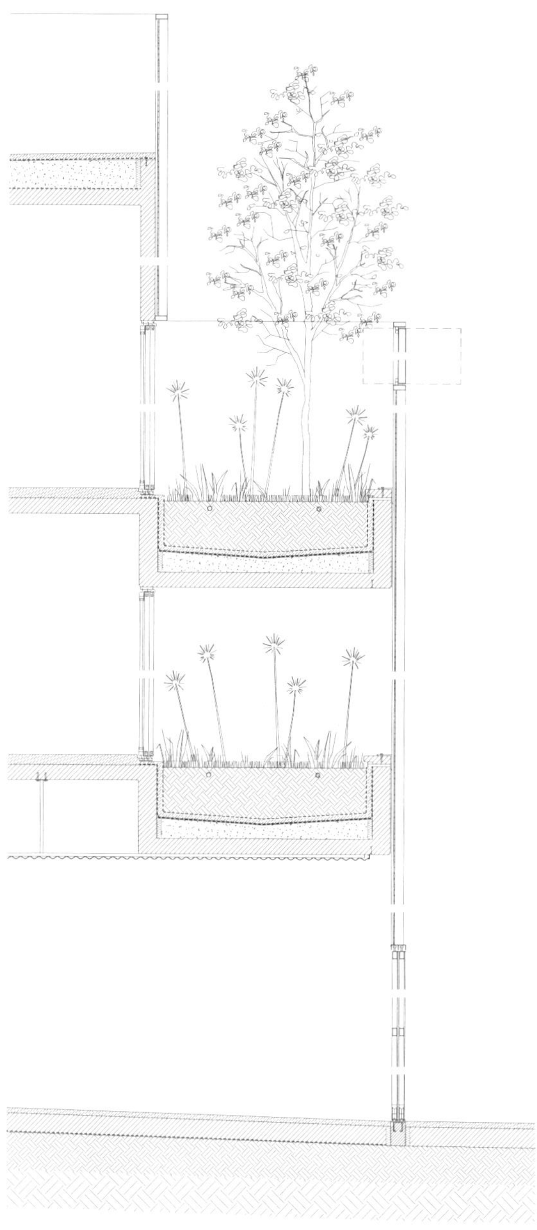

Bonpland 2169 building

Bonpland 2169 building

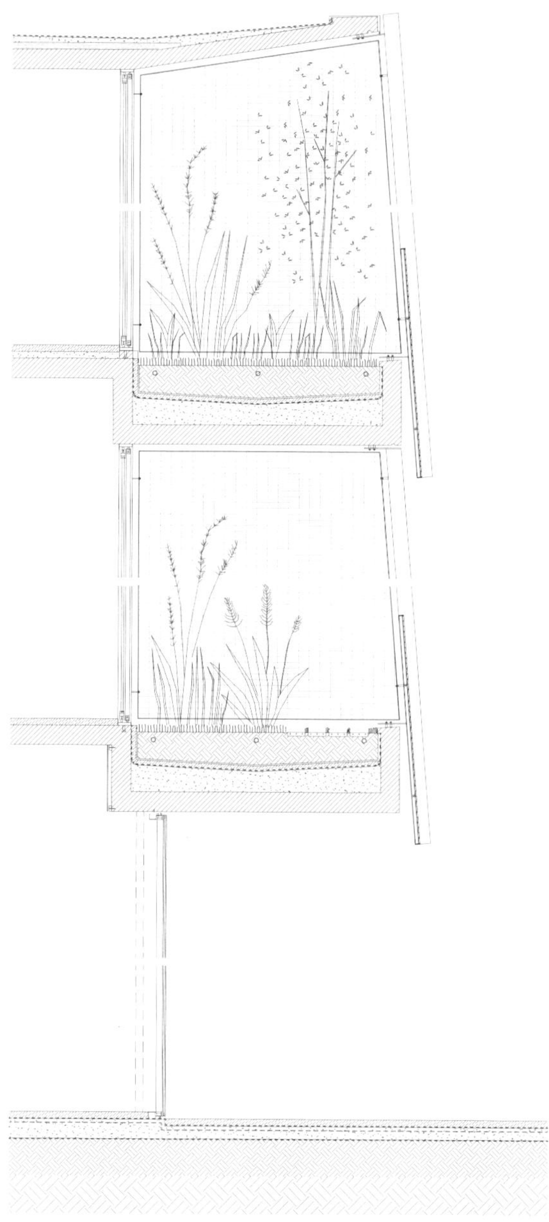

Puertos mixed-use complex

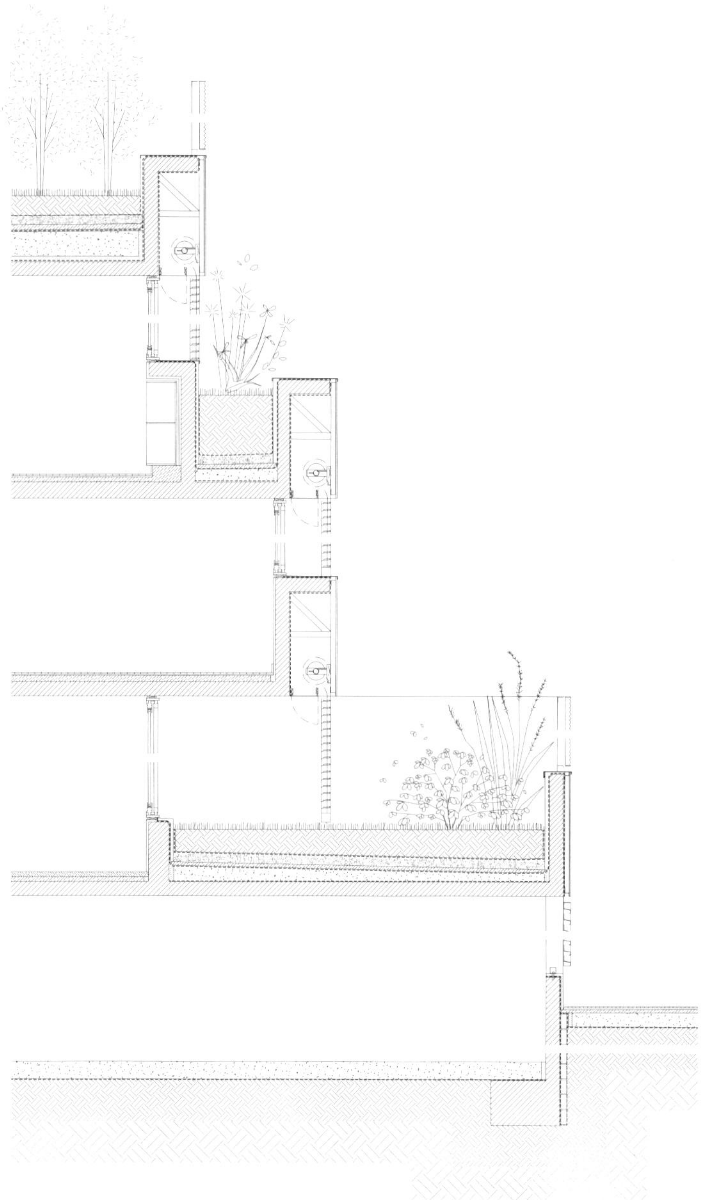

La vecindad Plaza Mafalda building

La vecindad Plaza Mafalda building

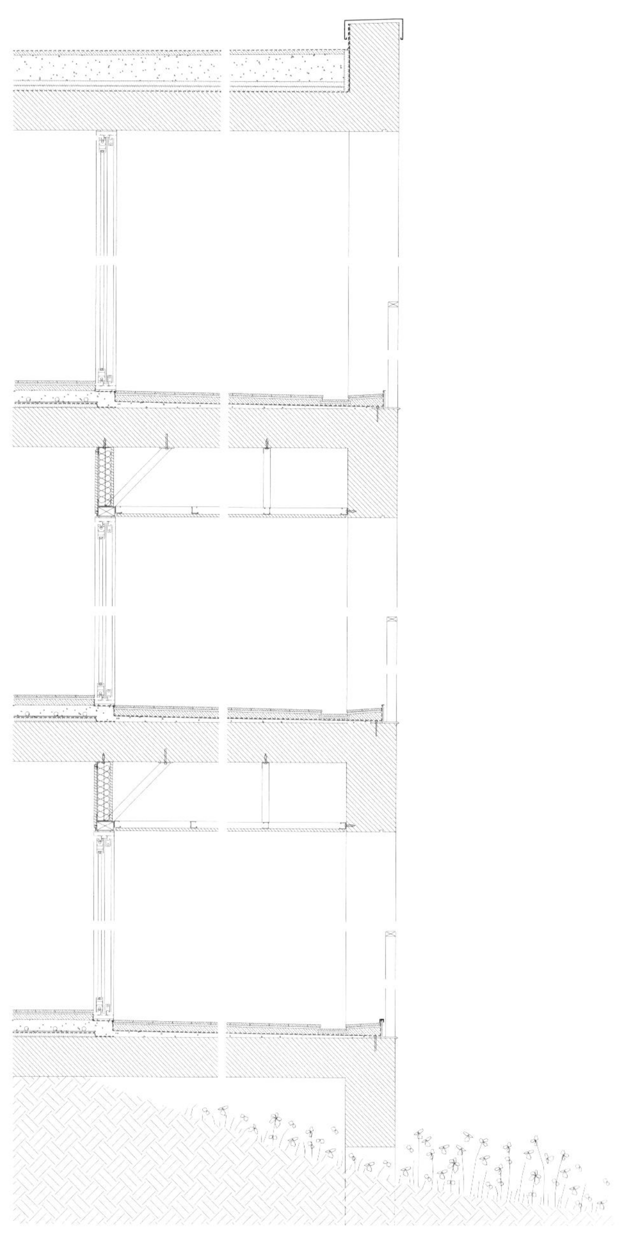

Puertos mixed-use complex

Puertos mixed-use complex

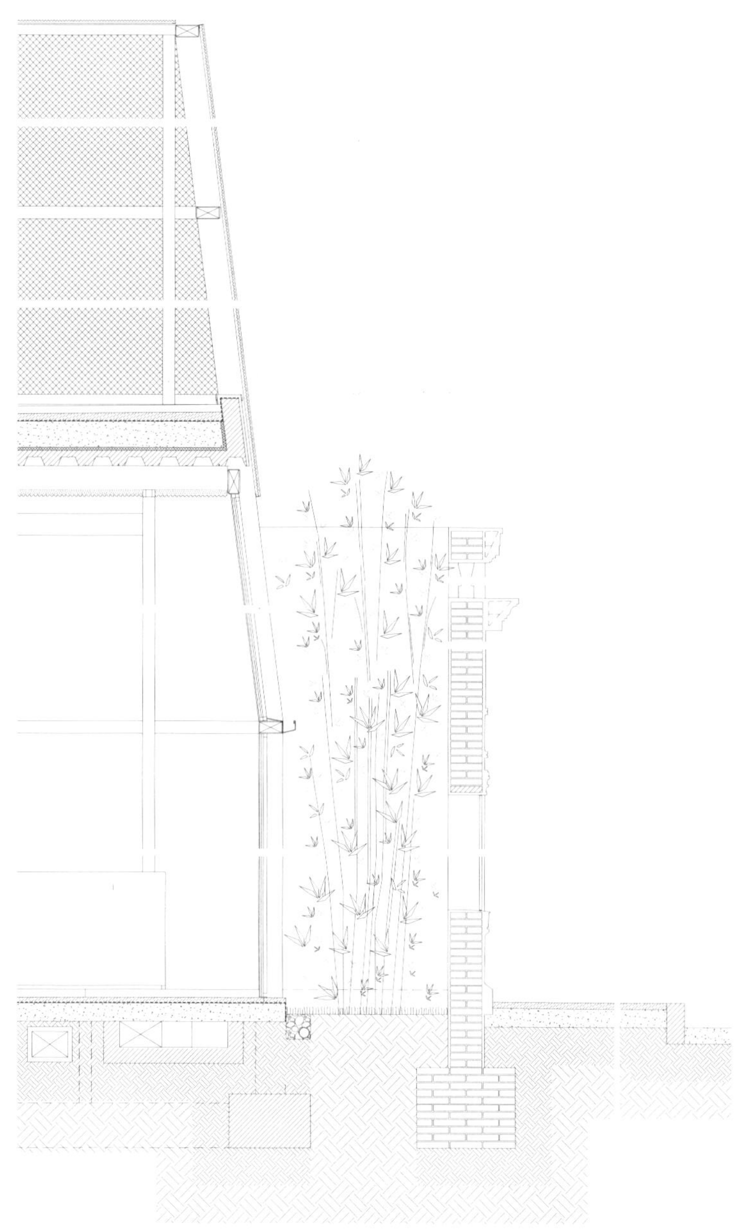

Orno pizzeria

Orno pizzeria

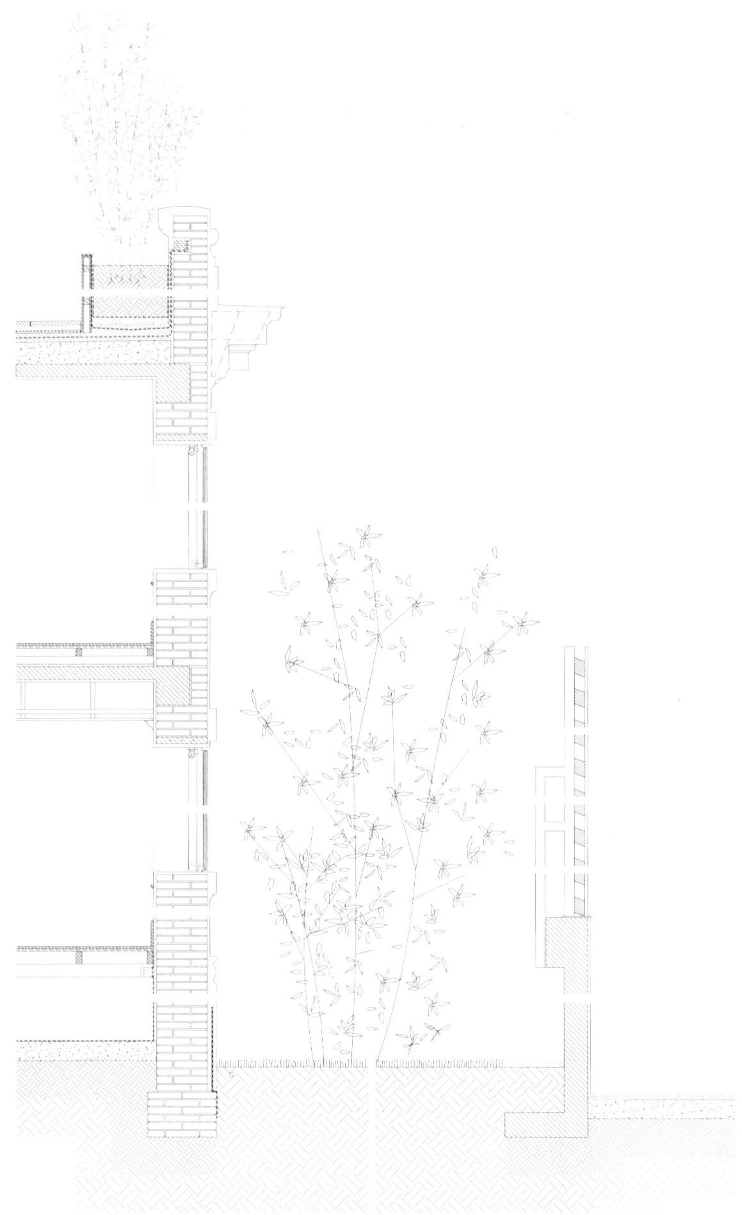

Embassy of the Republic of Philippines extension

Embassy of the Republic of Philippines extension

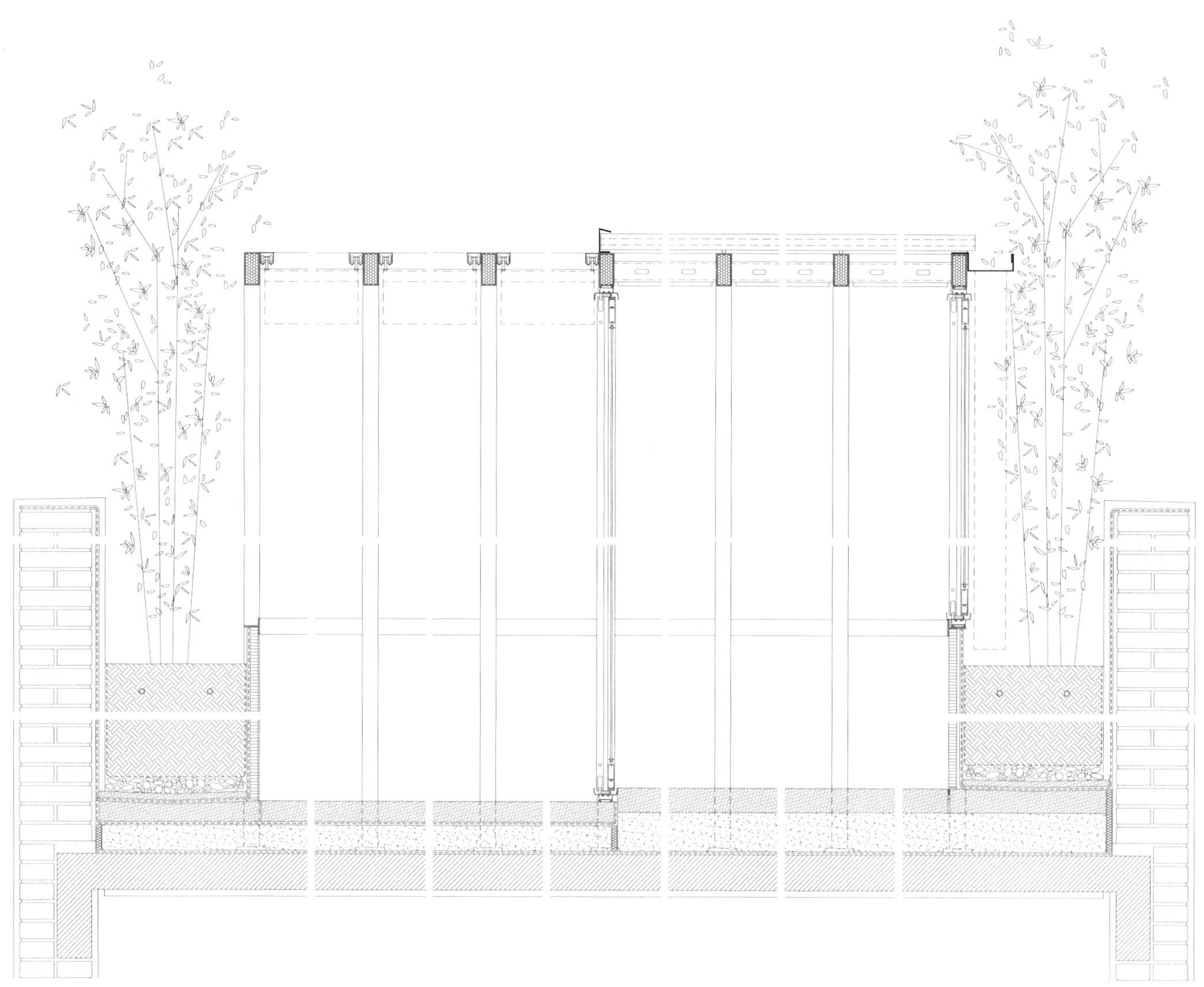

Piñeiro house extension

Piñeiro house extension

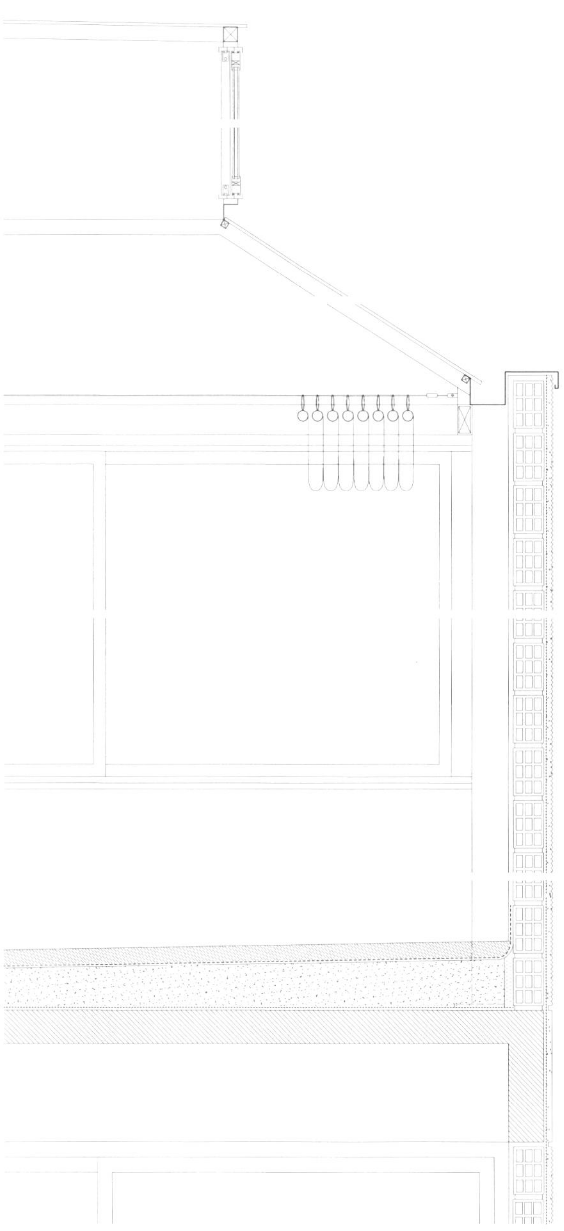

33 Orientales 138 extension

33 Orientales 138 extension

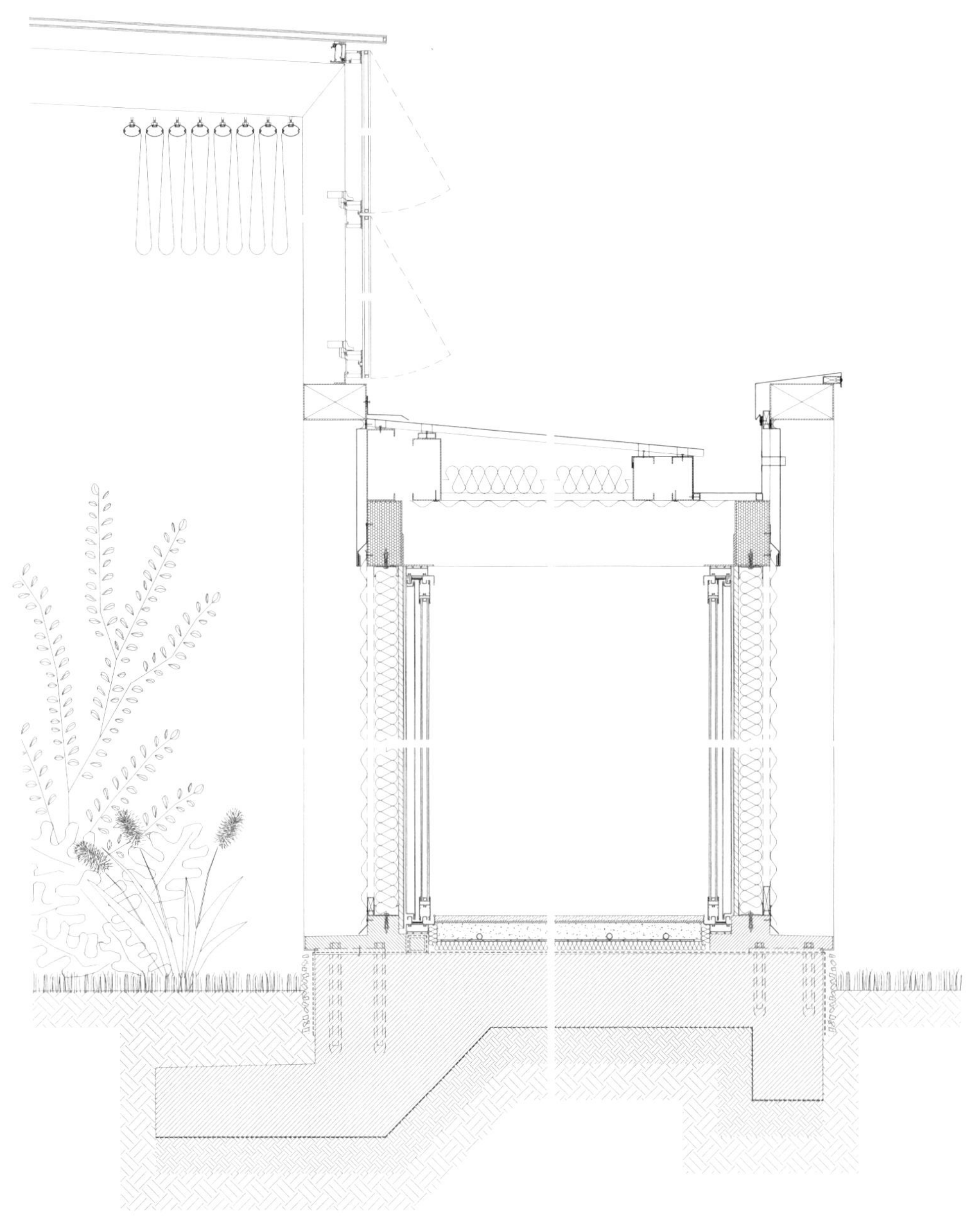

Cepé house

Cepé house

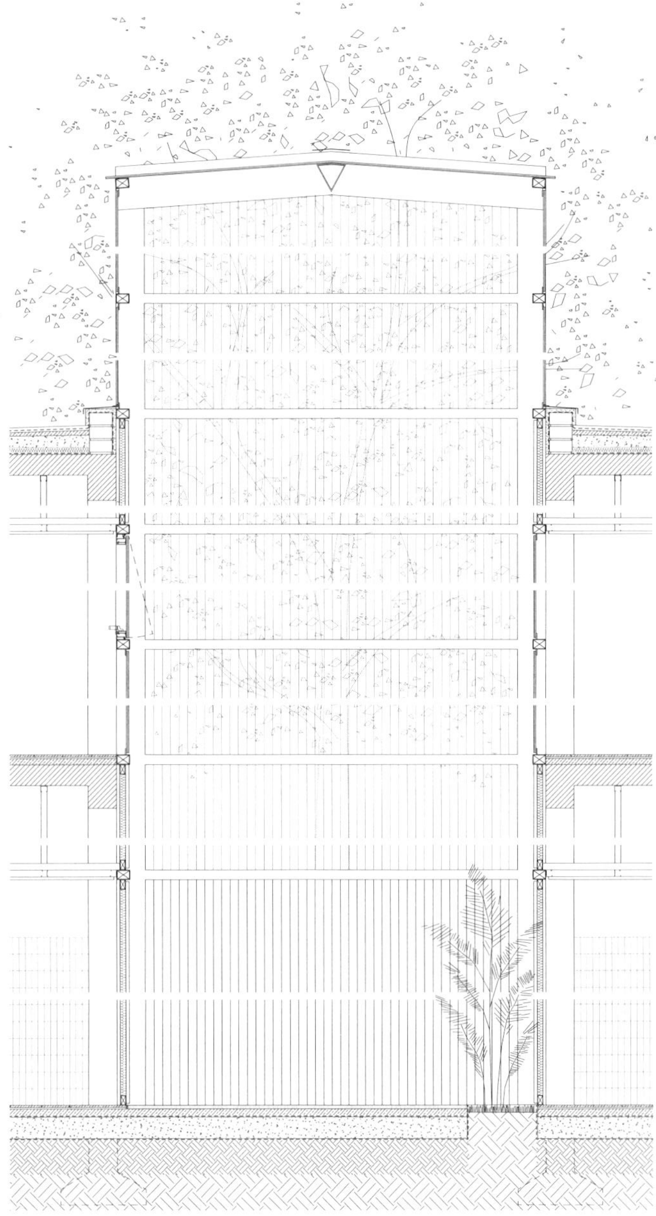

Guayaquil 650 veterinary clinic

Guayaquil 650 veterinary clinic

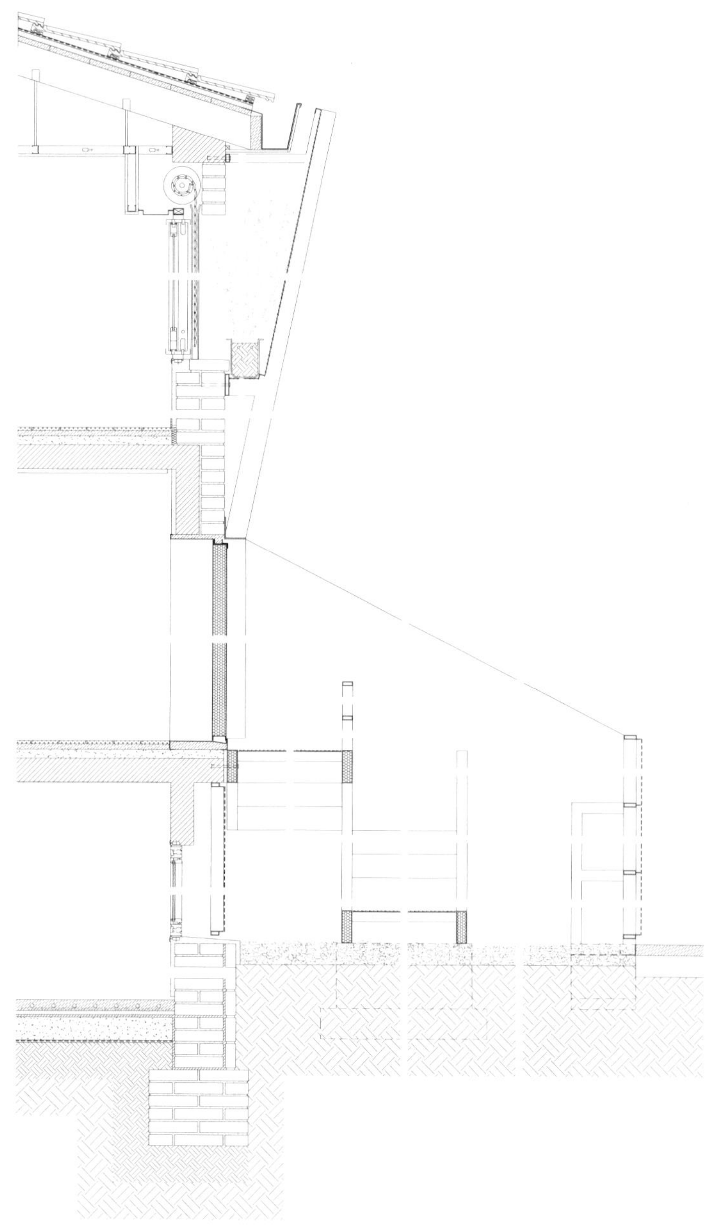

Fernández house extension

Fernández house extension

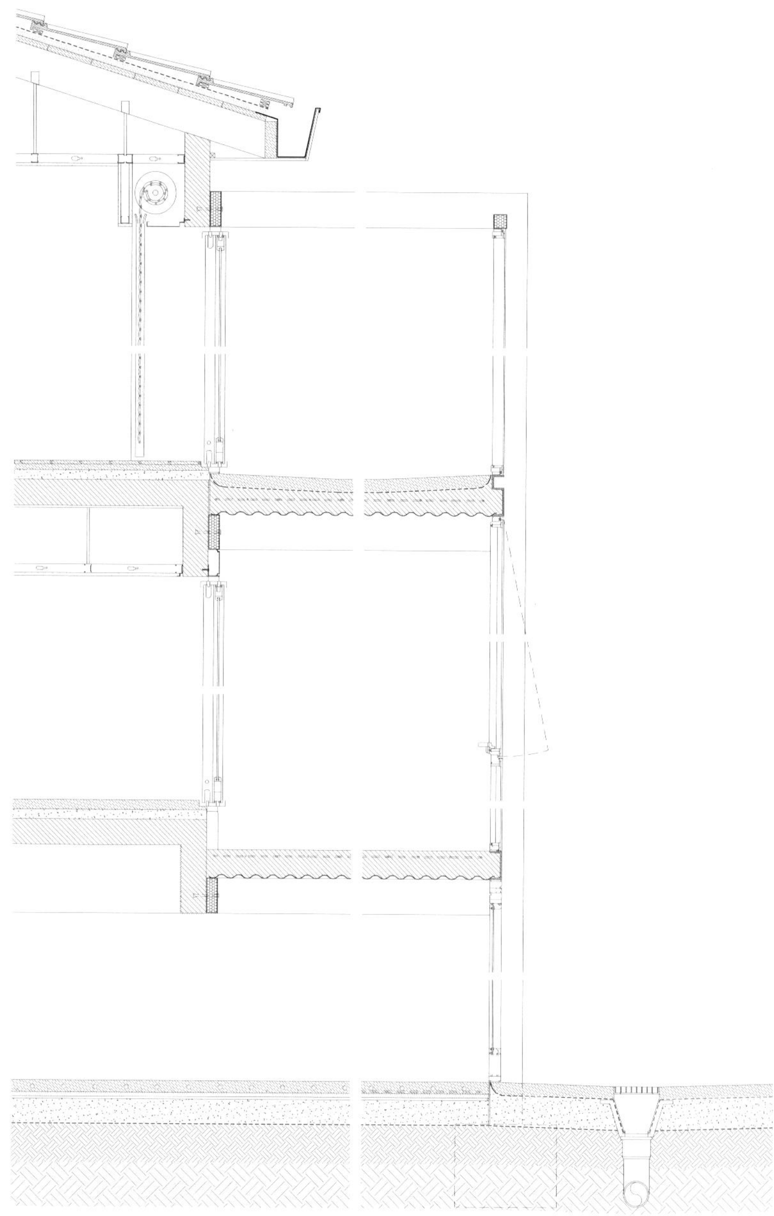

Fernández house extension

Fernández house extension

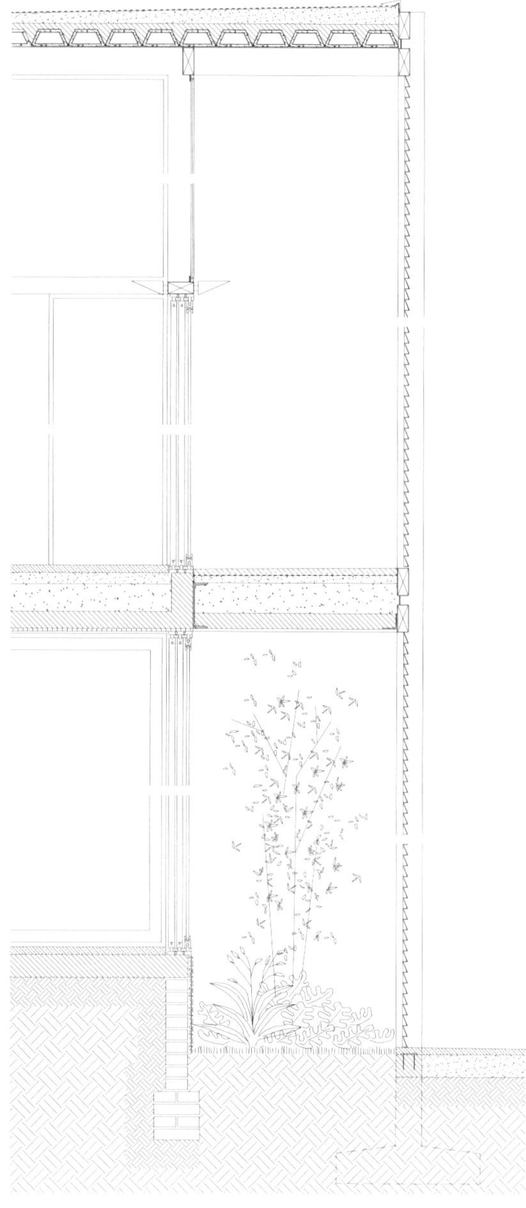

Bernardello house extension

Bernardello house extension

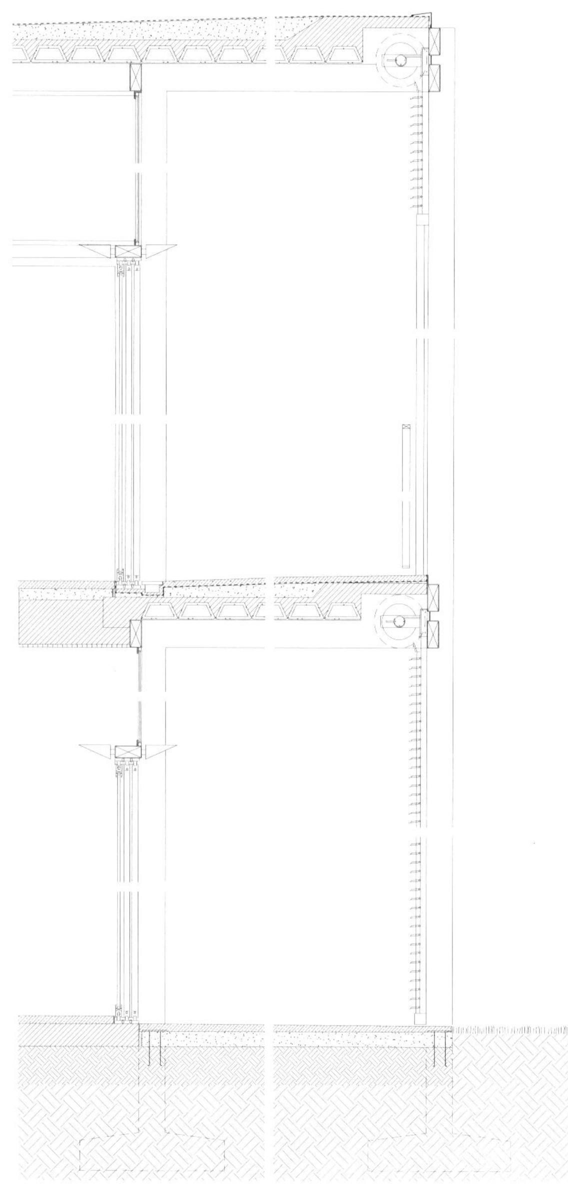

Bernardello house extension

Bernardello house extension

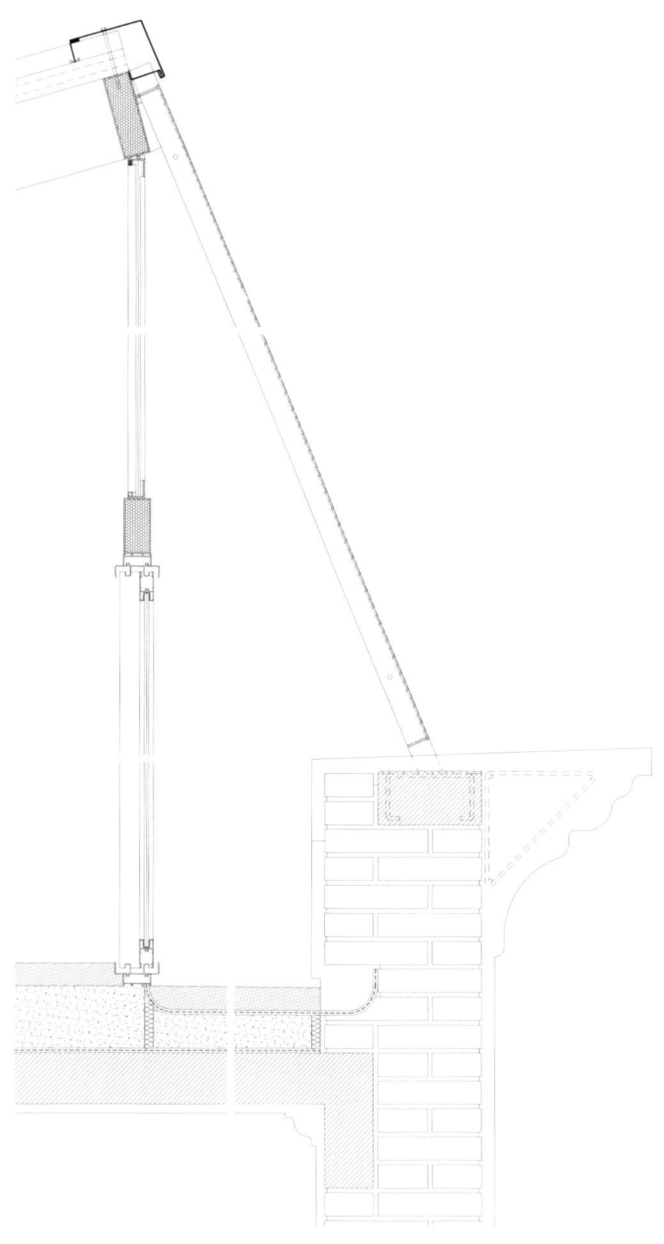

Blas house extension

Blas house extension

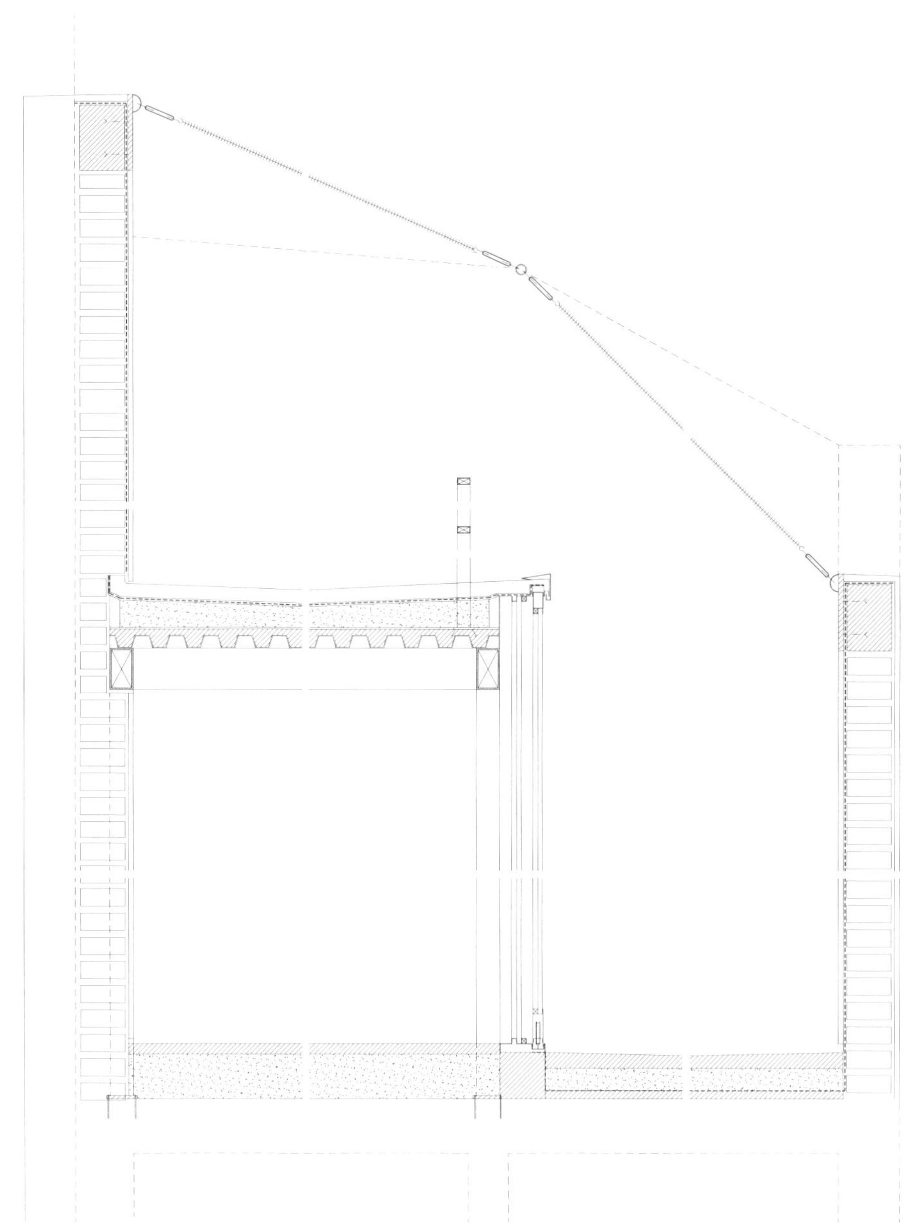

Núñez house extension

Núñez house extension

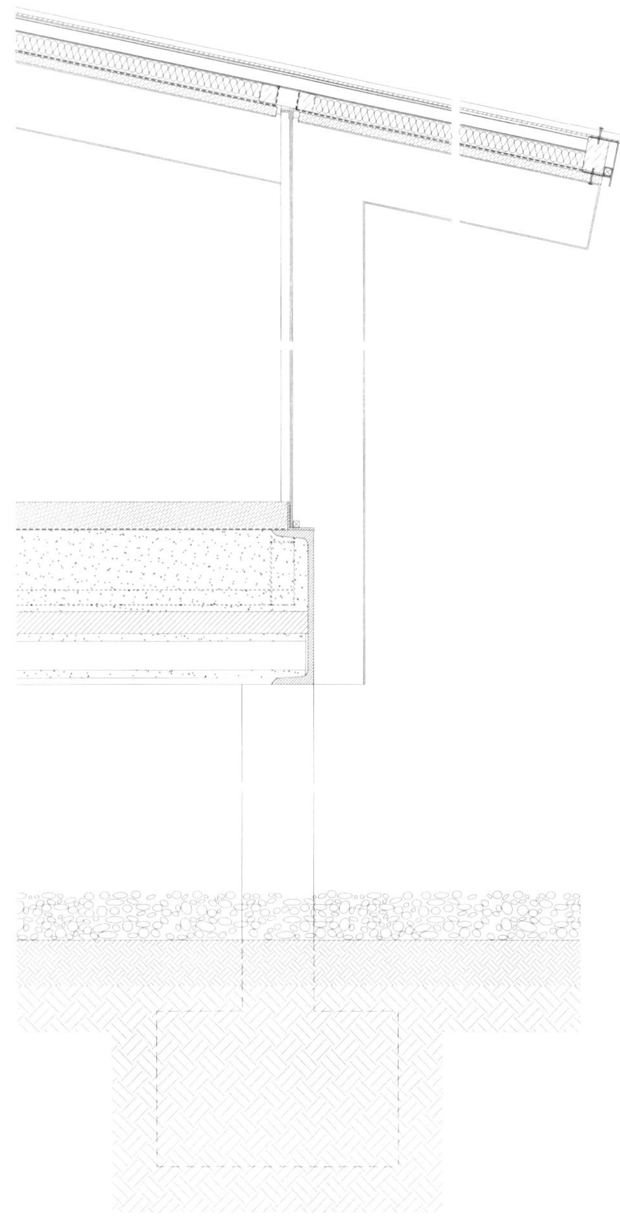

Macchi house extension

Macchi house extension

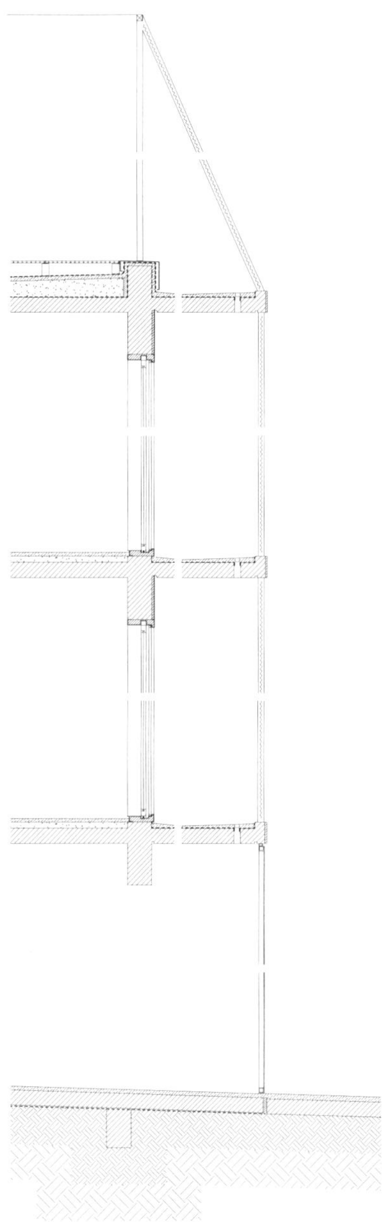

Lago houses

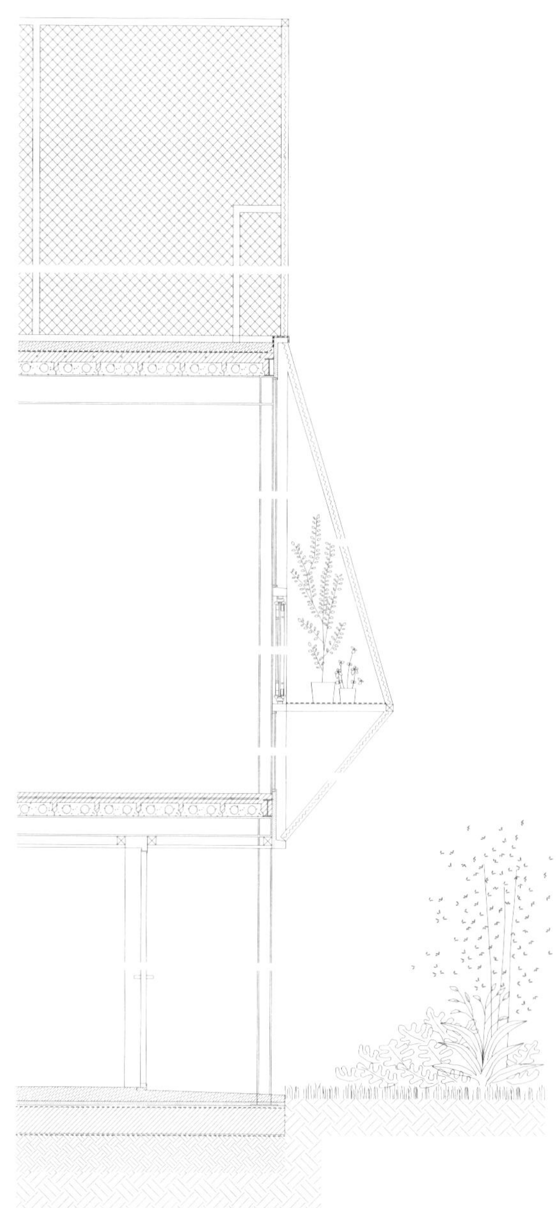

Martos house

Martos house

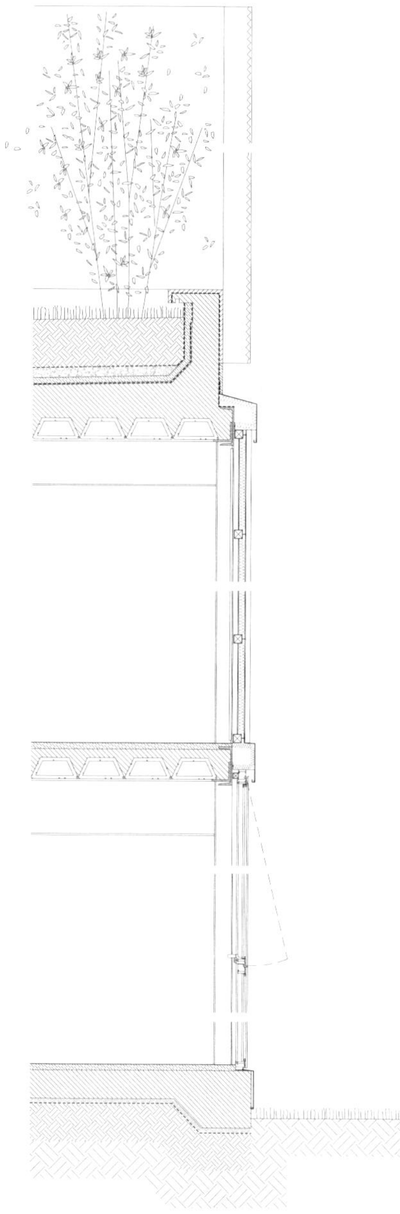

Hydro Industrial pavilion

Hydro Industrial pavilion

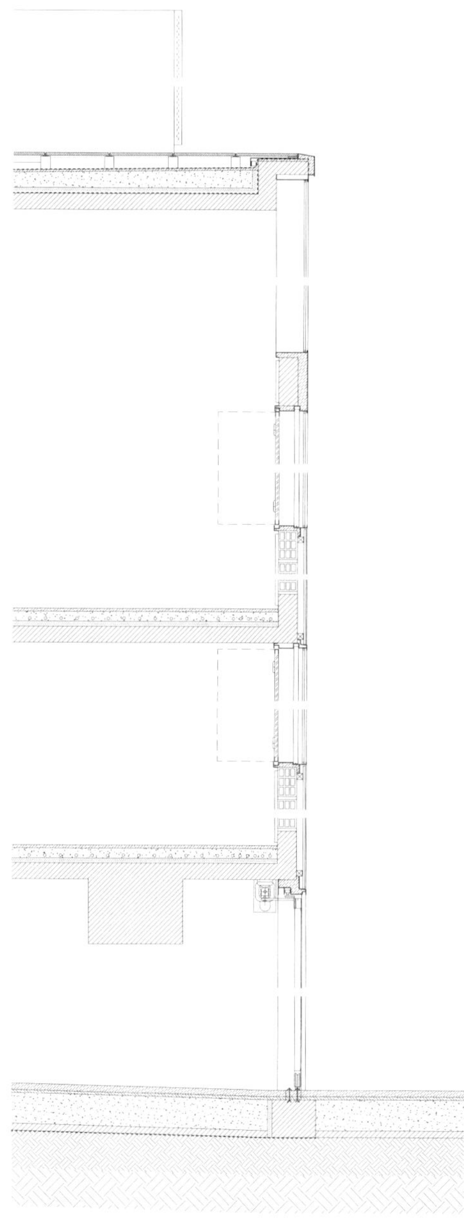

Conesa 4560 building

Conesa 4560 building

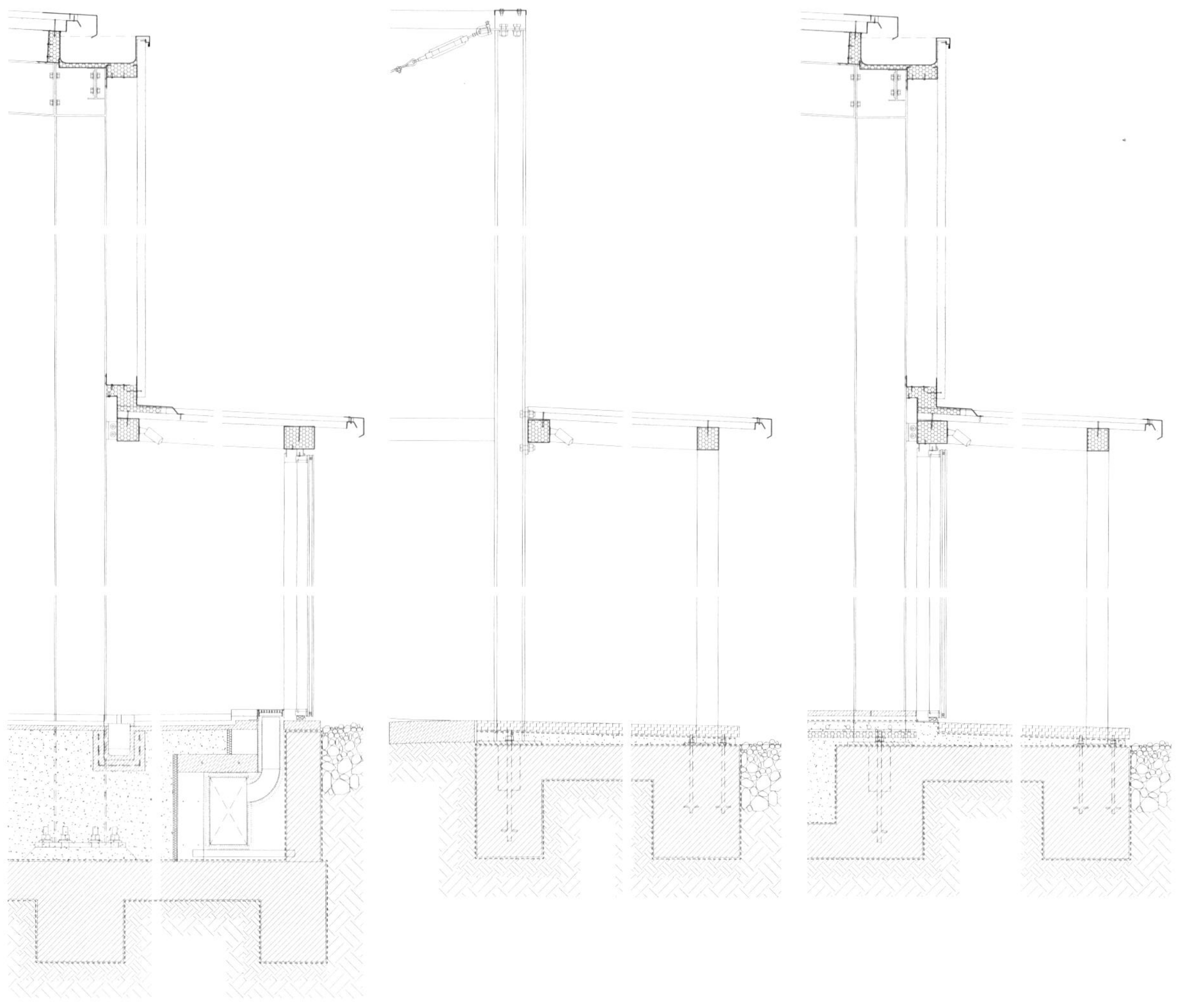

Puertos sports club

Puertos sports club

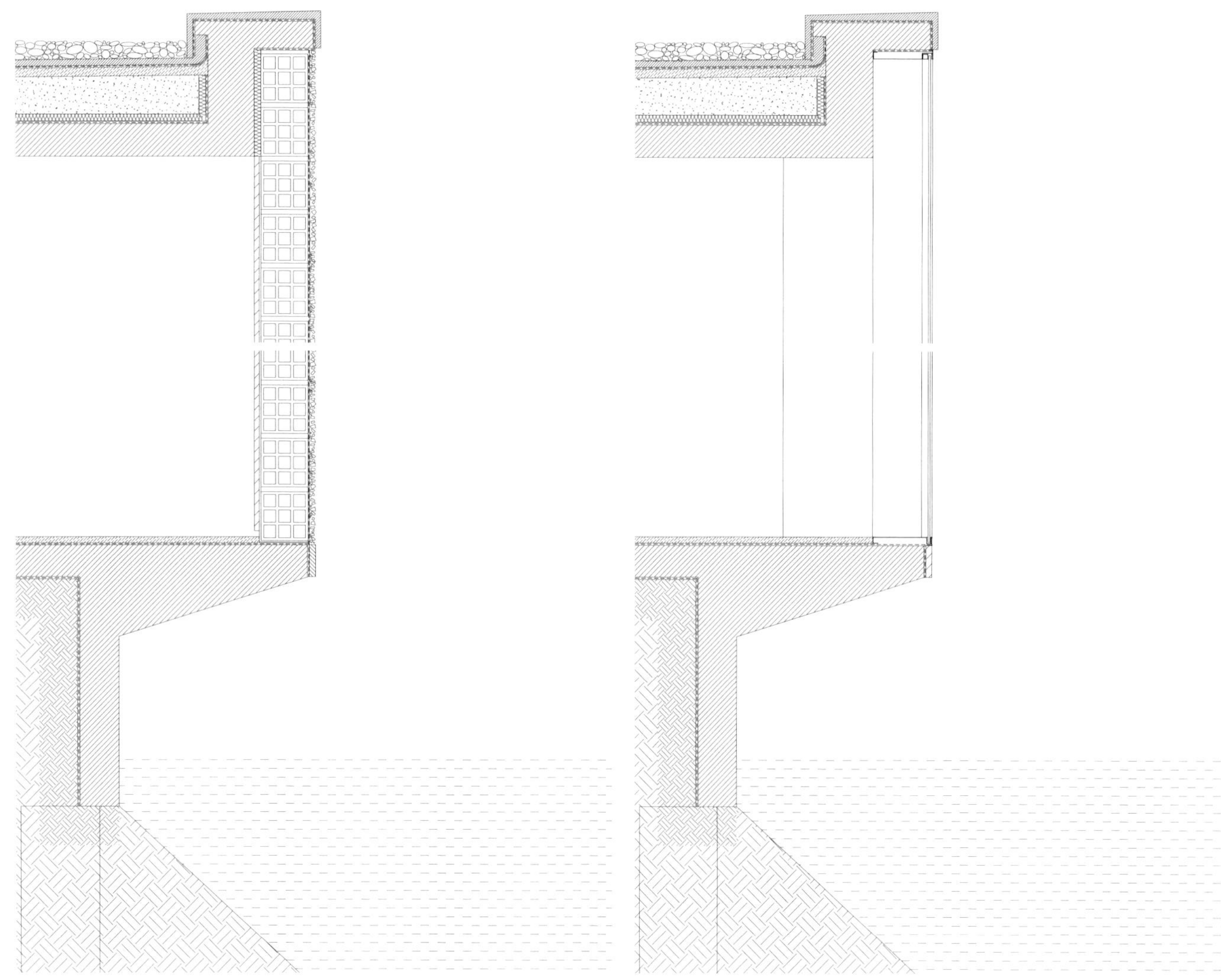

La Cándida club house

La Cándida club house

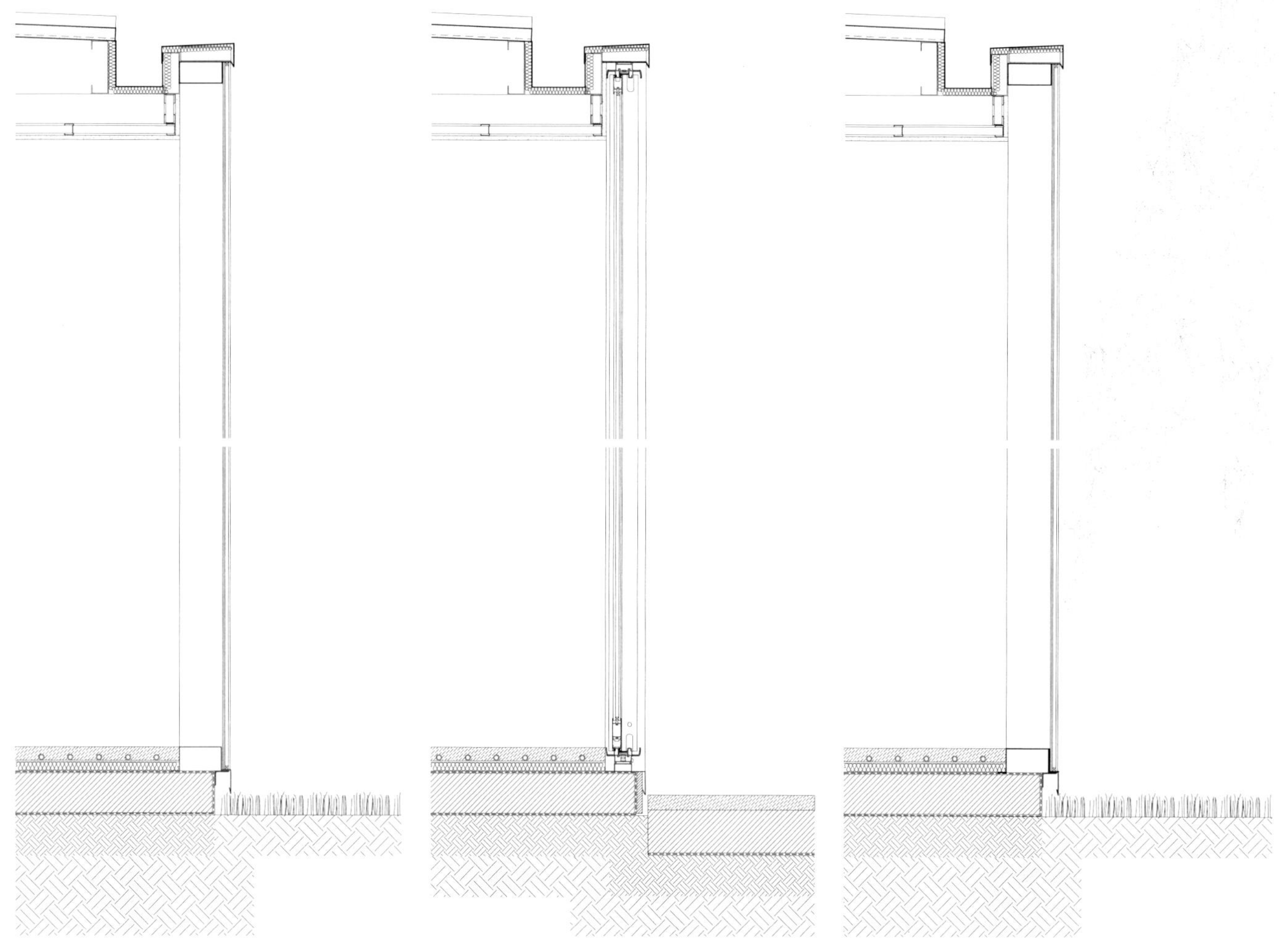

Sáenz house

Sáenz house

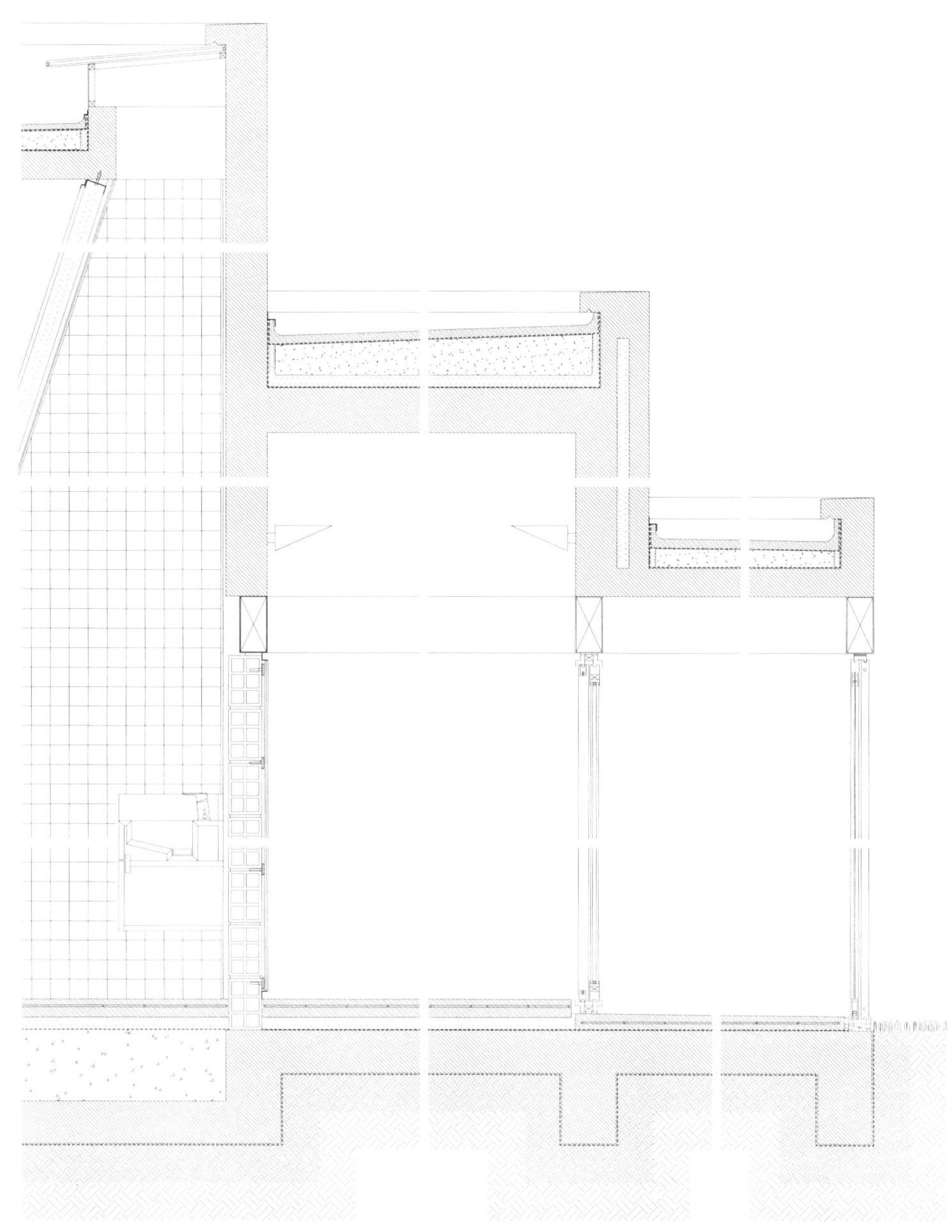

Nuñez house

Nuñez house

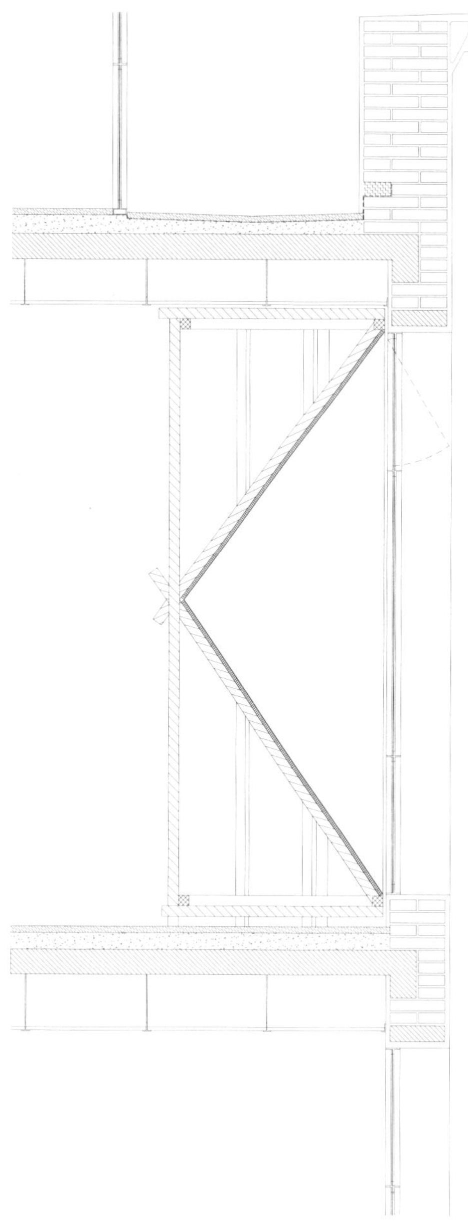

O que vemos, o que nos olha

The Work of Others

We like to think our work is based on an interest in the work of others. What makes it specific to our time, to our place, or even to our persons is contingent and secondary in terms of that opening statement. We couldn't describe it on the basis of these variables because we understand them as such. Maybe that's why we restrict ourselves to describing a single possible constant, a single invariable: our continued interest in the work of others. Paradoxically, it is in the construction of this constellation that we find the finest refuge for our subjectivity.

But who are those we call "others", exactly?

Although it might appear self-evident, the origin of this attitude resides in the idea of sharing authorship with a second person. The use of our surnames – without mediations of any kind – to designate our studio emphasizes this idea.

Even so, what we understand by "others" has an even greater significance. Here, we are referring to the experiences of quite a few colleagues who, in their passage through the world, have left behind a body of work that has managed to outlive their presence. We are interested in understanding this work as a design material that does not differentiate between geographical or temporal limits. We observe the work of others as a material purified by the passage of time, on the basis of which we can construct a private landscape wide enough for our gaze to form unrepeatable, and therefore unique, relationships.

And running parallel to this immaterial construction, this conversation lacking in active interlocutors, the work of others appears inscribed within the here and now.

We are interested in imagining part of a second conversation that only manages to have meaning if it is maintained simultaneously with other colleagues, precisely with those who share the idea that the construction of knowledge is a collective task. A conversation in which it is not necessary to maintain an excessive closeness. Just the opposite, in fact. We are referring to a type of exchange that calls for actors who are conscious of their position, however temporary it may be, so they can be sensitive to the arguments of others.

In closing, it would be unfair not to mention that, hidden within this constant, external insistence, there is a private desire that is forward-looking, the wish for some interlocutor who is capable of understanding individual work as a new design material waiting to be re-described. In that respect we could claim that one of our greatest aspirations in relation to our work is that, at a certain moment, it might go on to form part of what we insist on calling "the work of others".

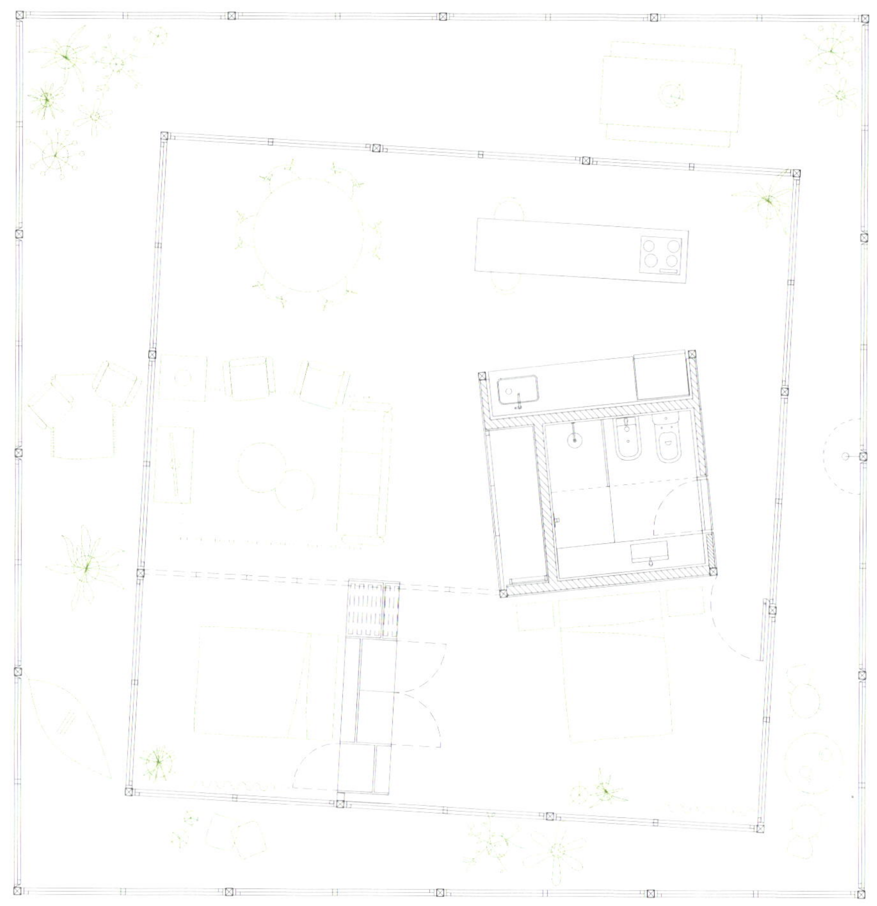

Núñez house

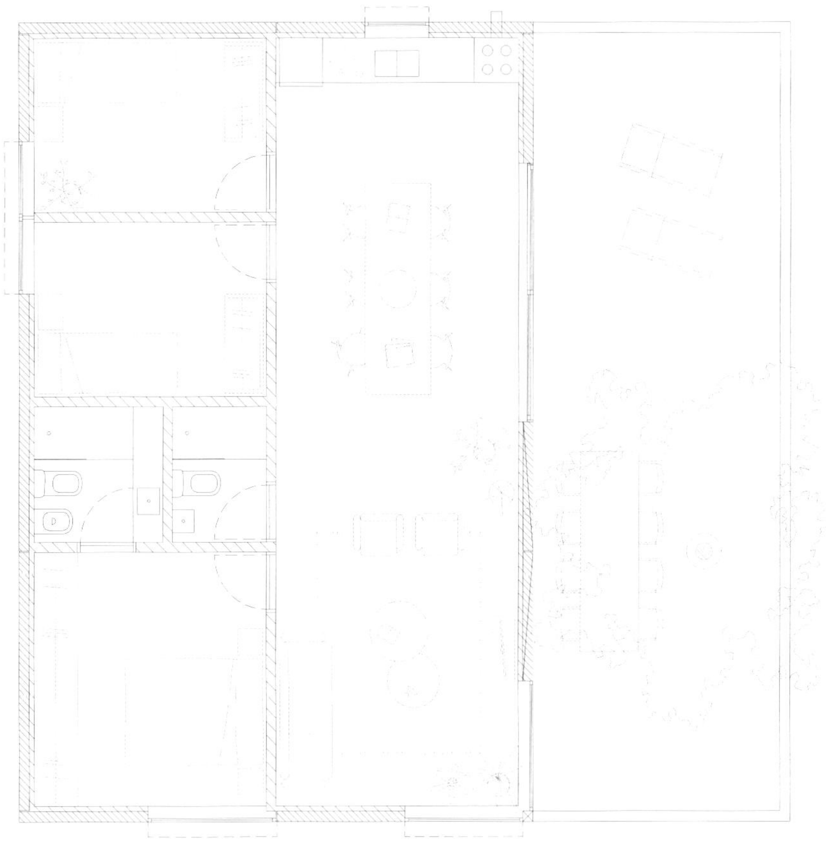

Figueroa house

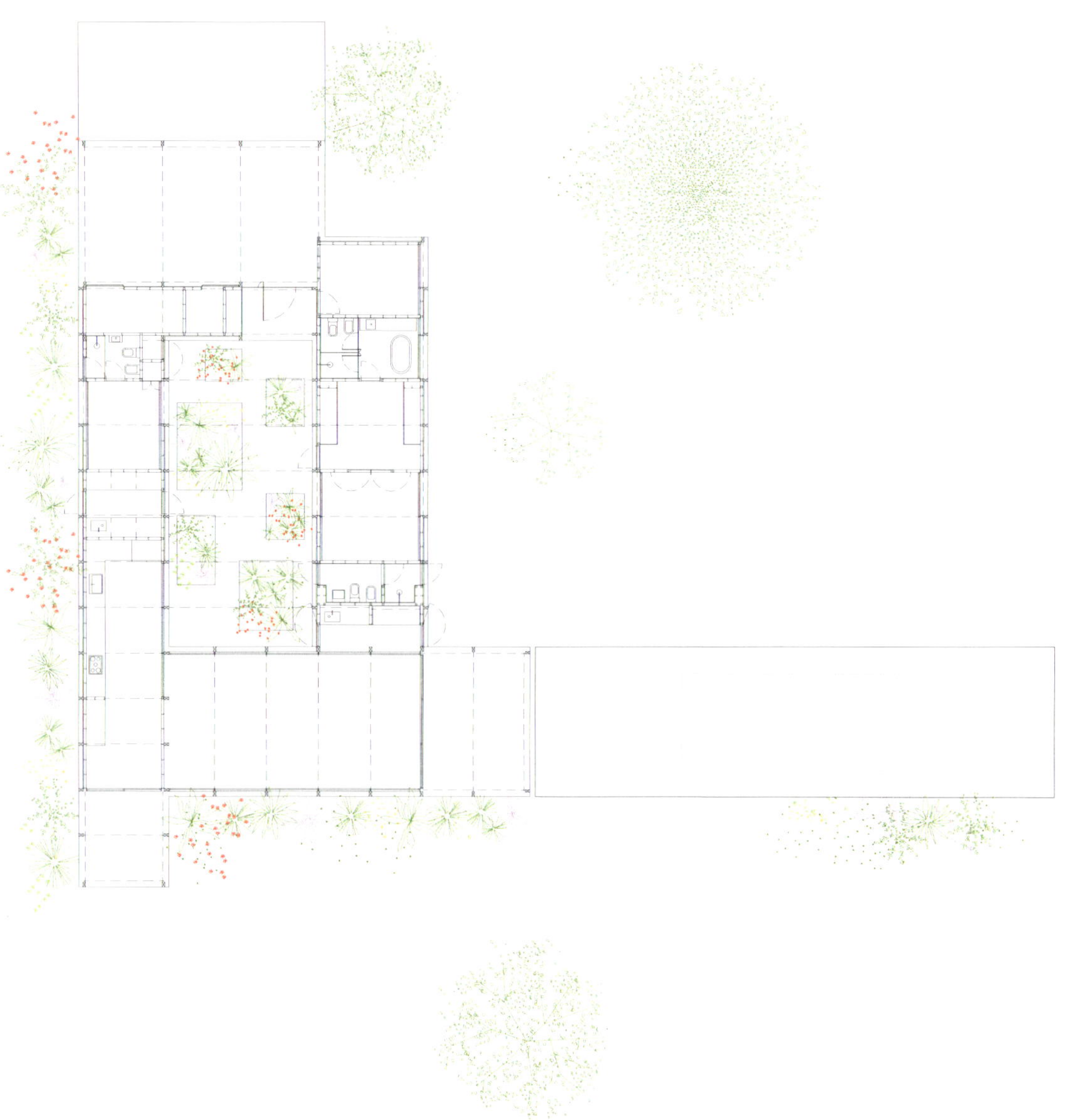

Cepé house

Sáenz house

Piñeiro house extension

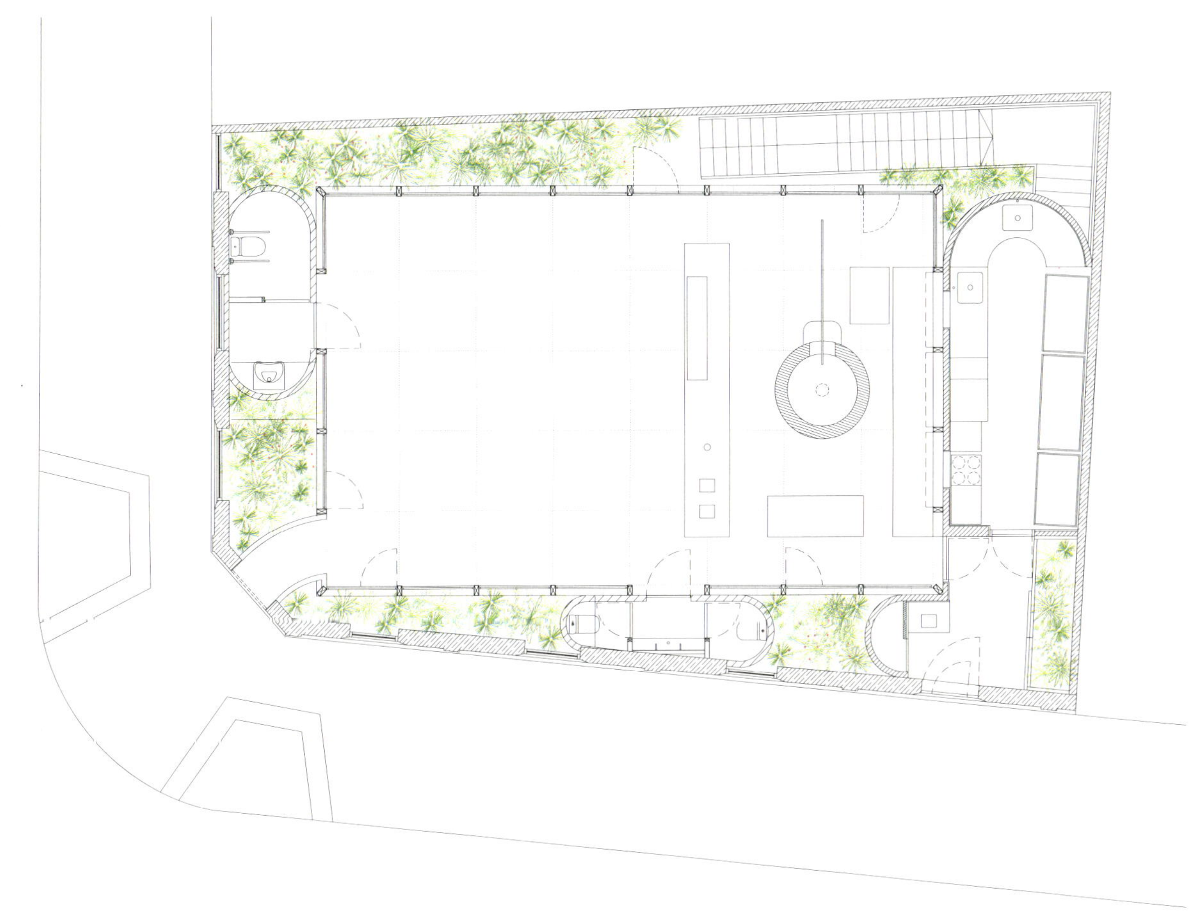

Orno pizzeria

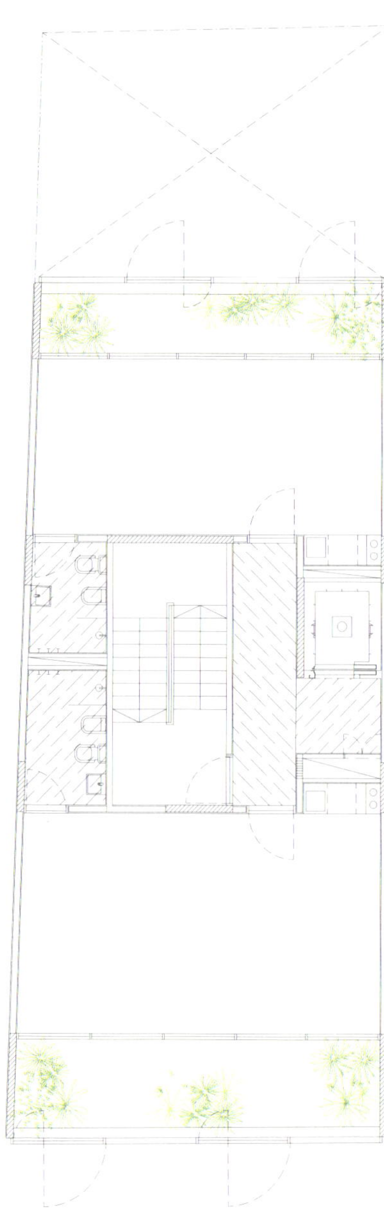

Bonpland 2169 building

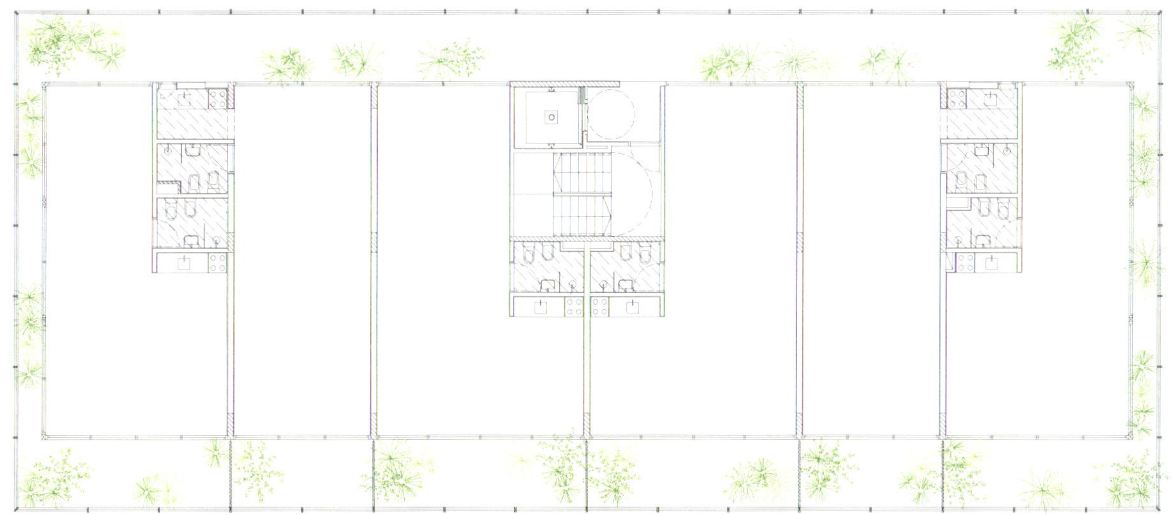

Puertos mixed-use complex

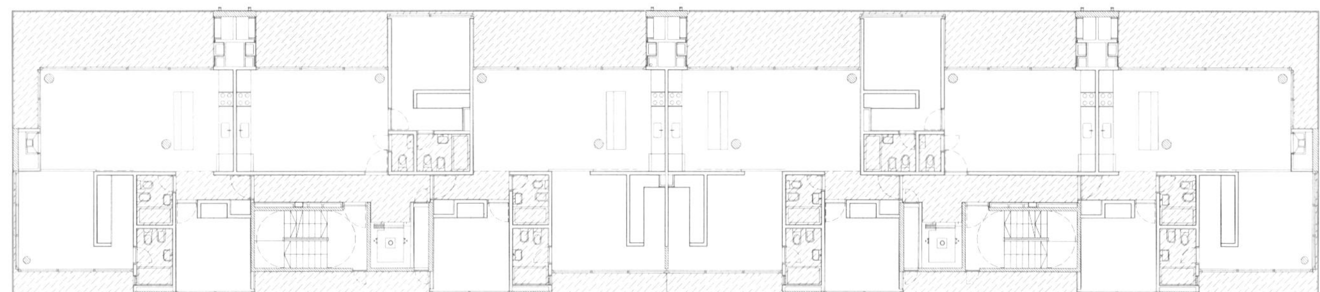

Puertos mixed-use complex

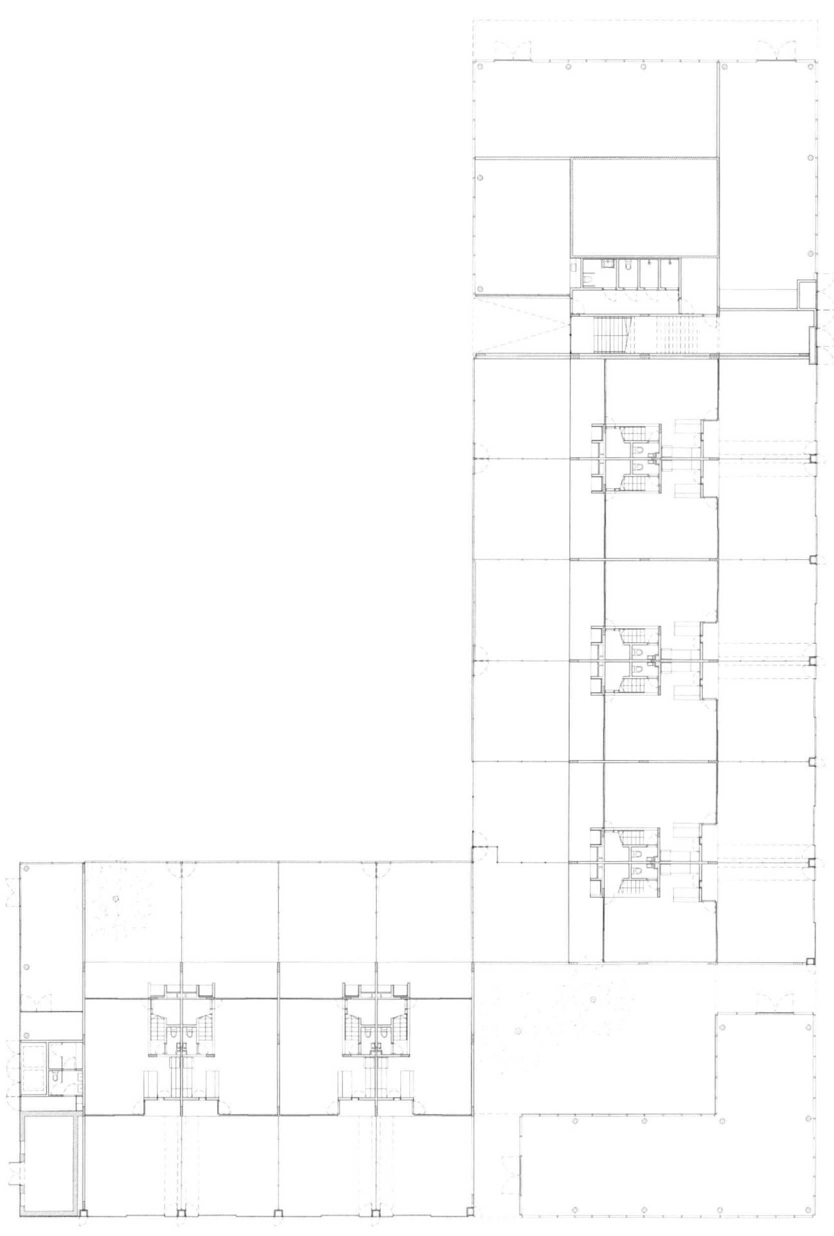

Puertos mixed-use complex

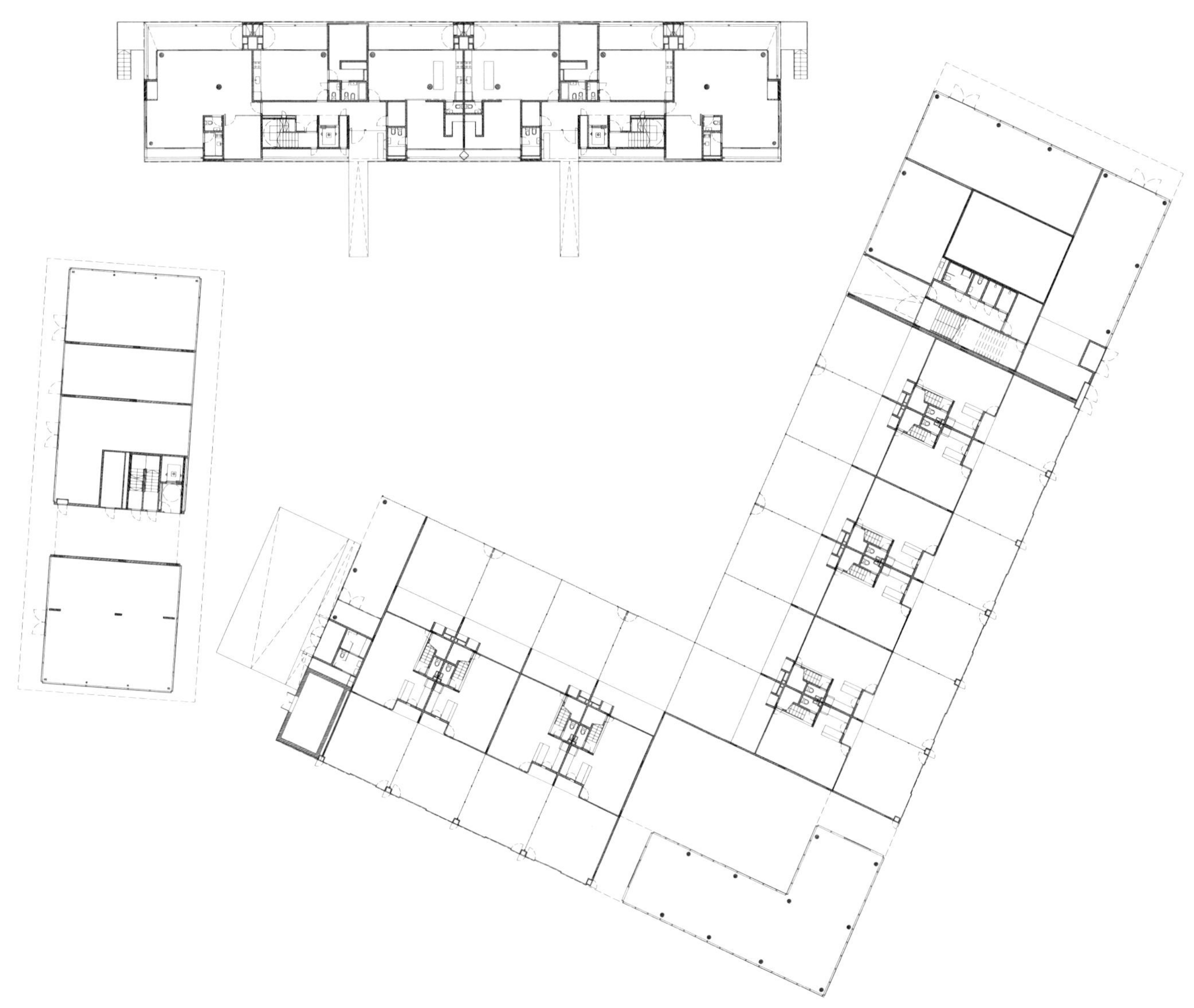

Puertos mixed-use complex

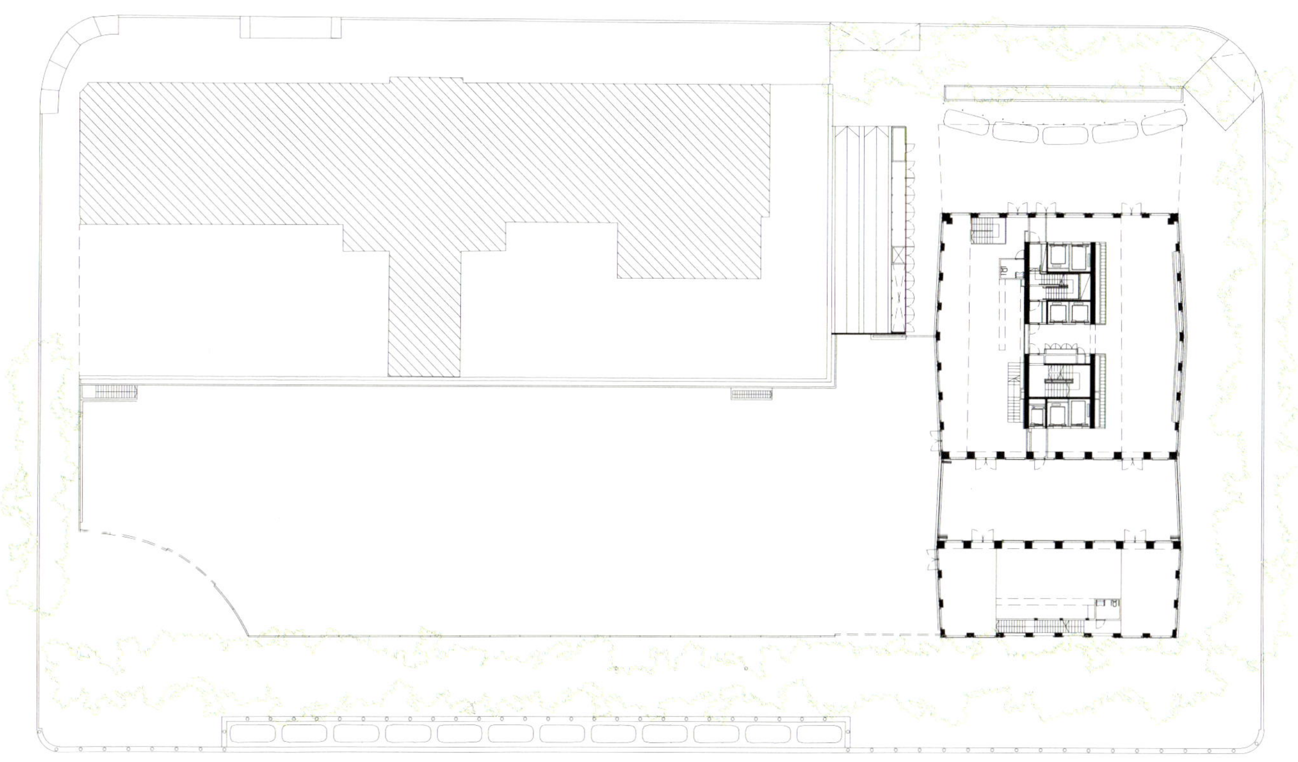

Huergo 475 tower

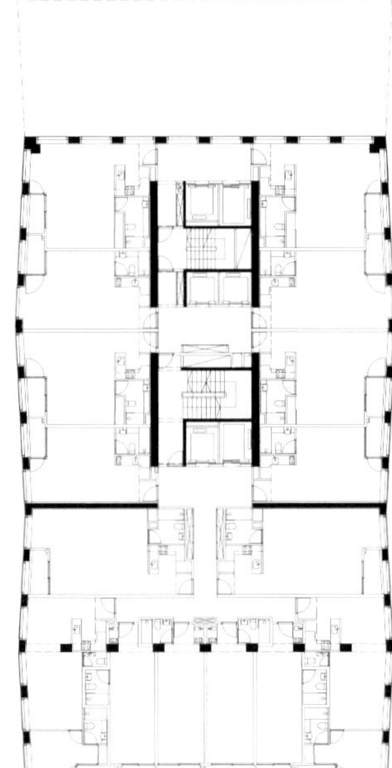

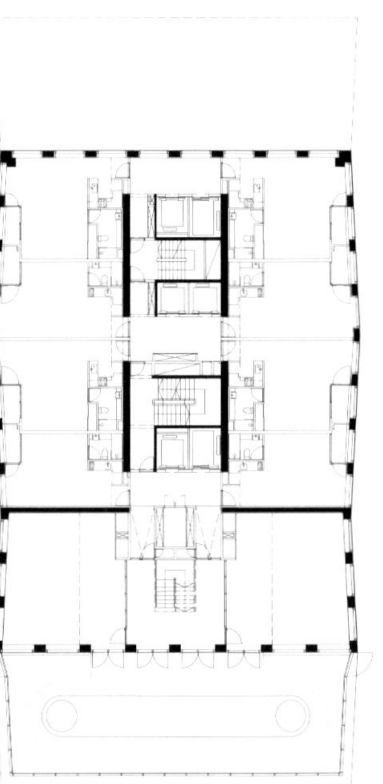

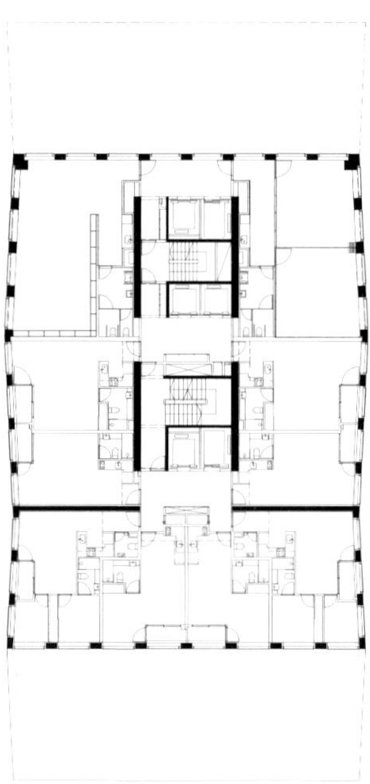

Huergo 475 tower

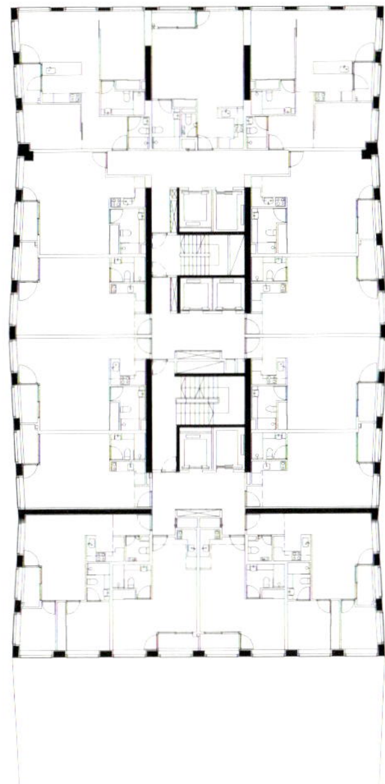
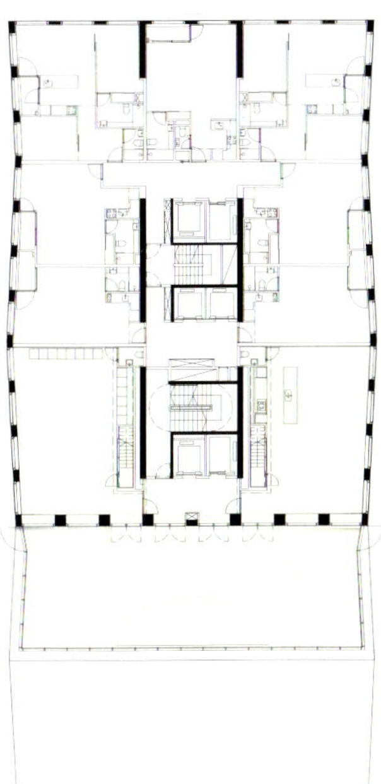
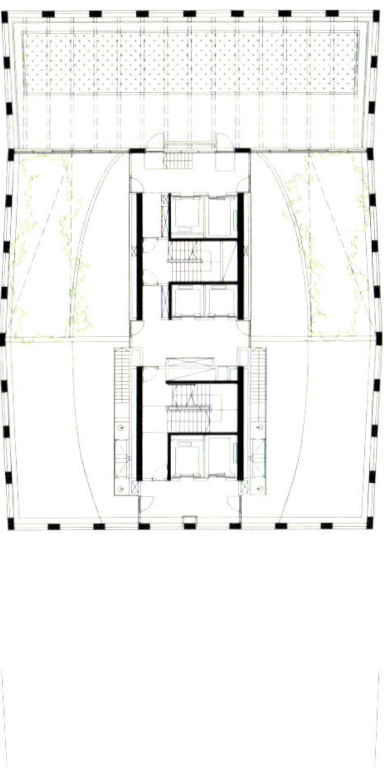

Huergo 475 tower

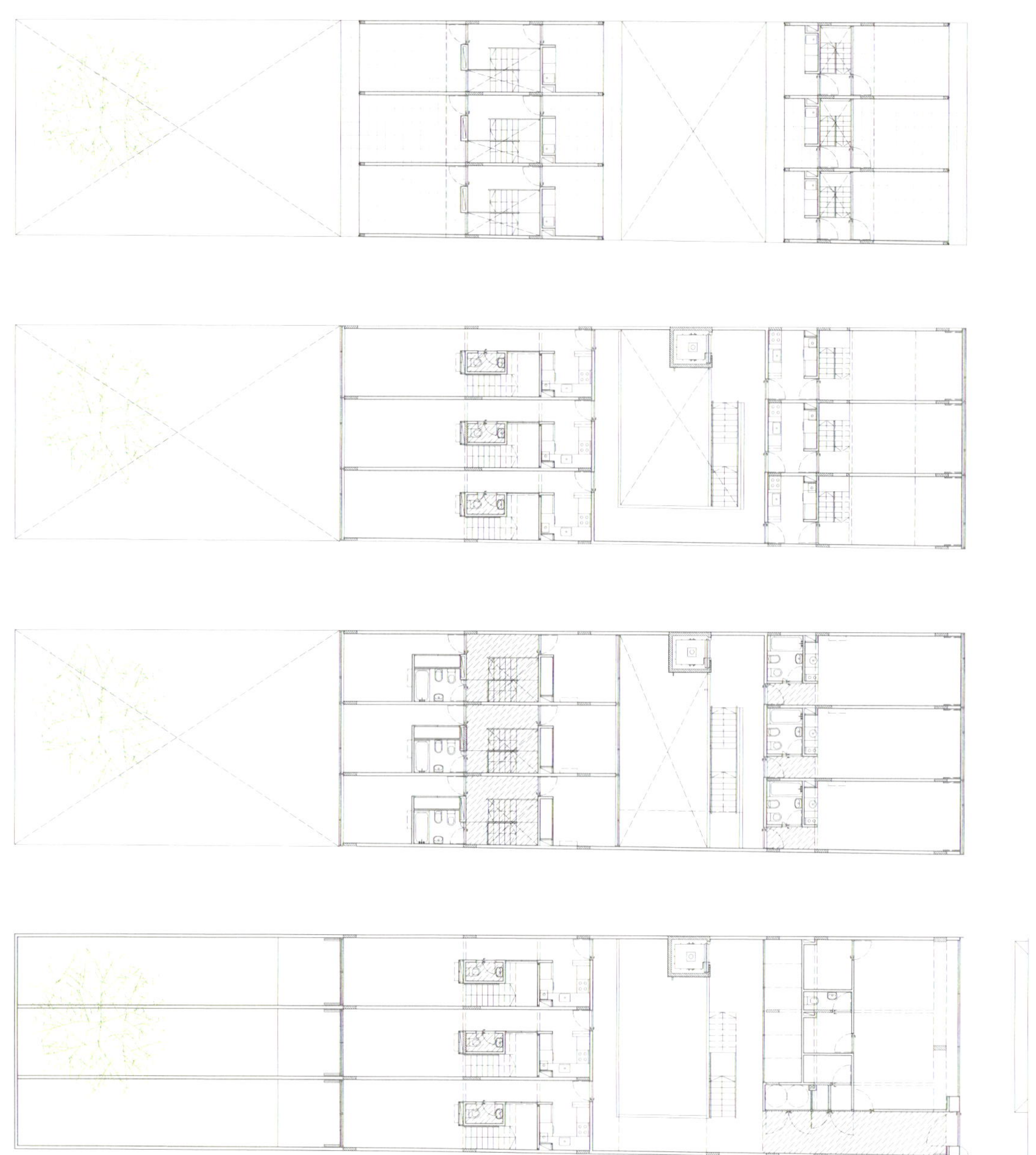

Conesa 4560 building

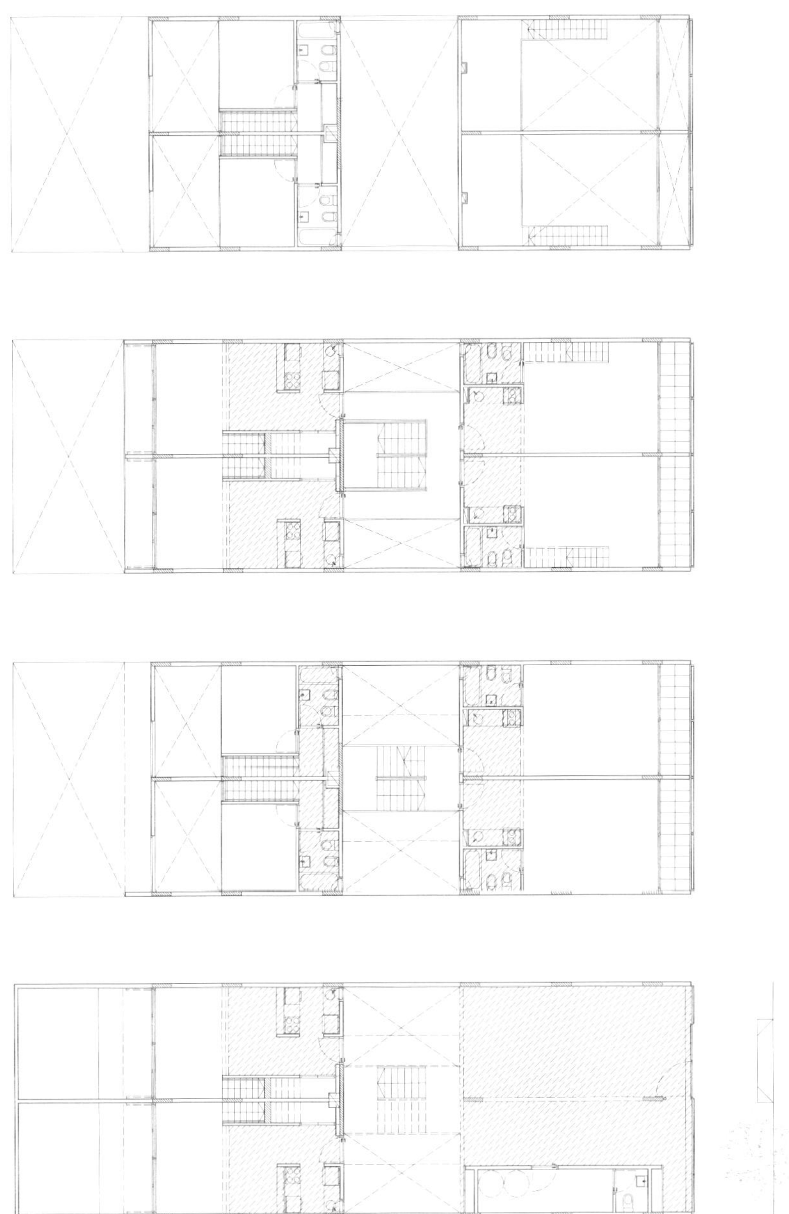

Arribeños 3182 building

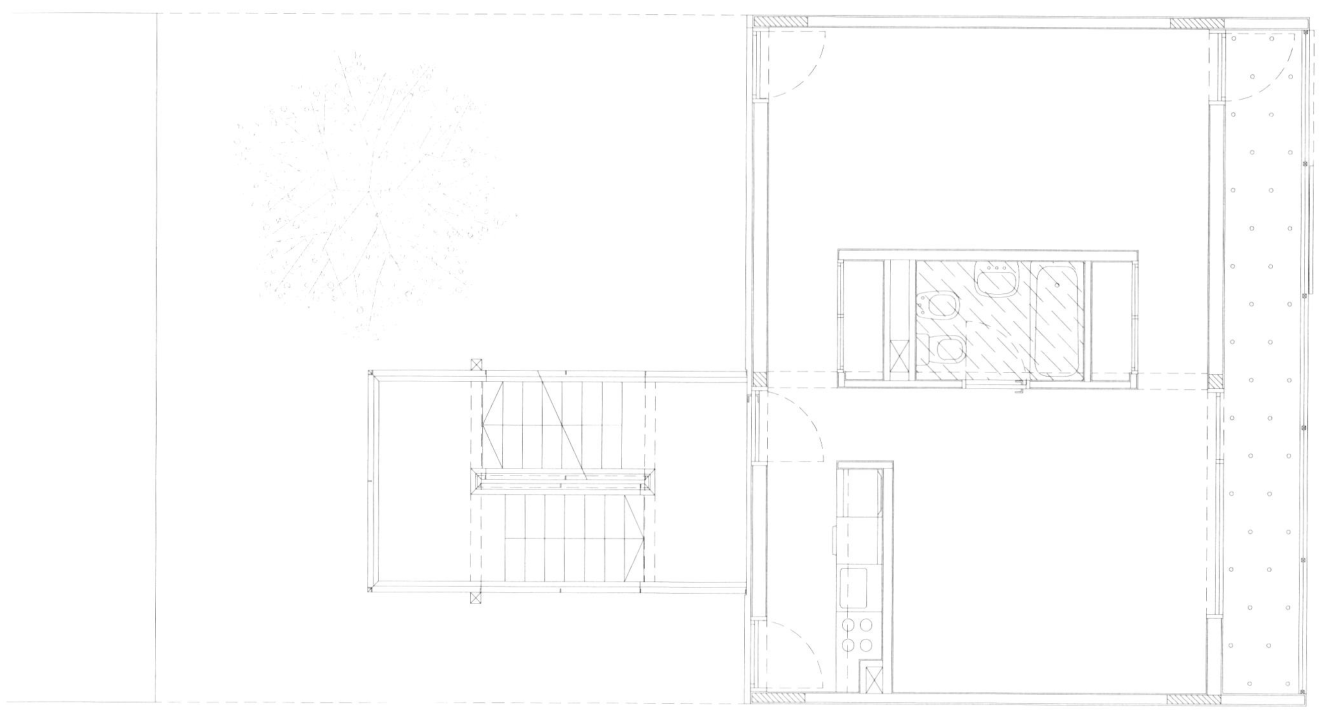

Lago houses

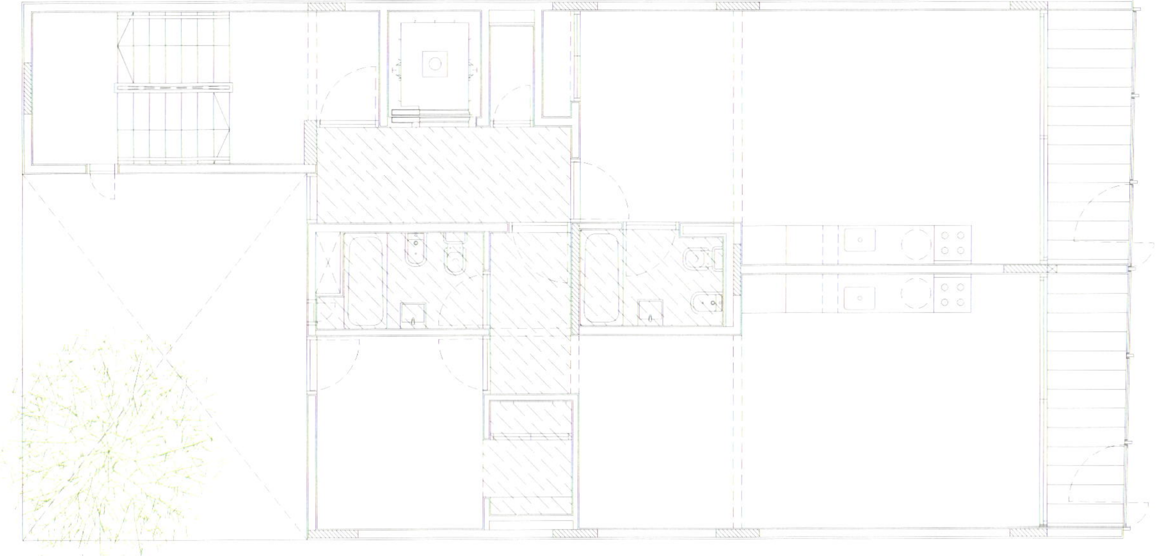

33 Orientales 138 building

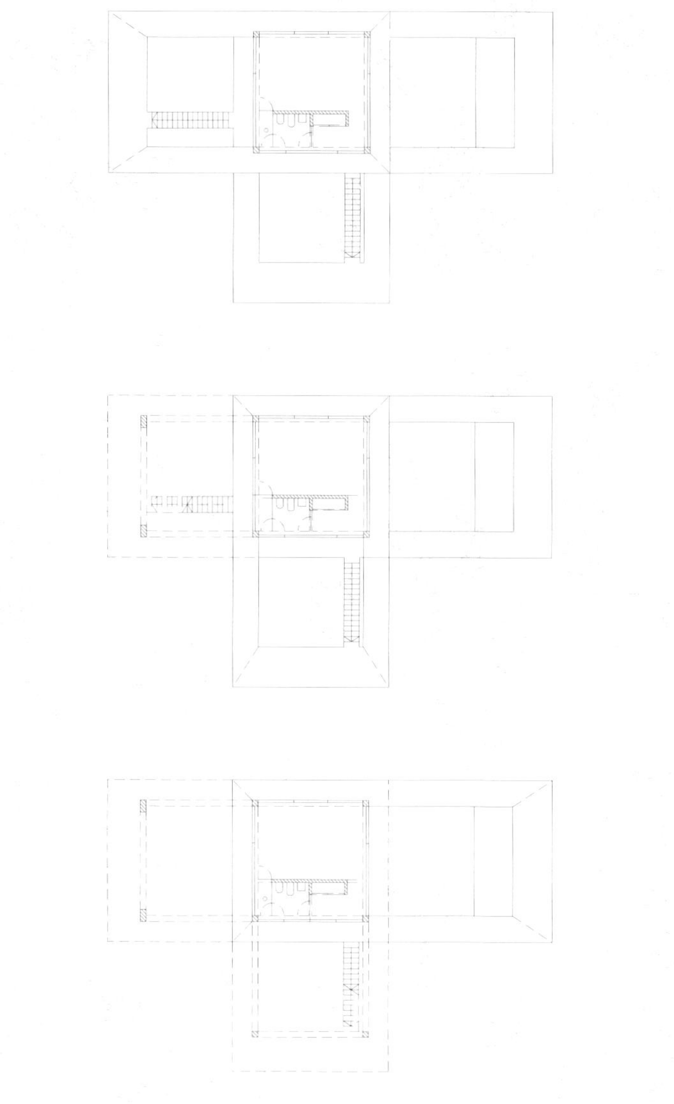

Eco tourism tower

Puertos sports club

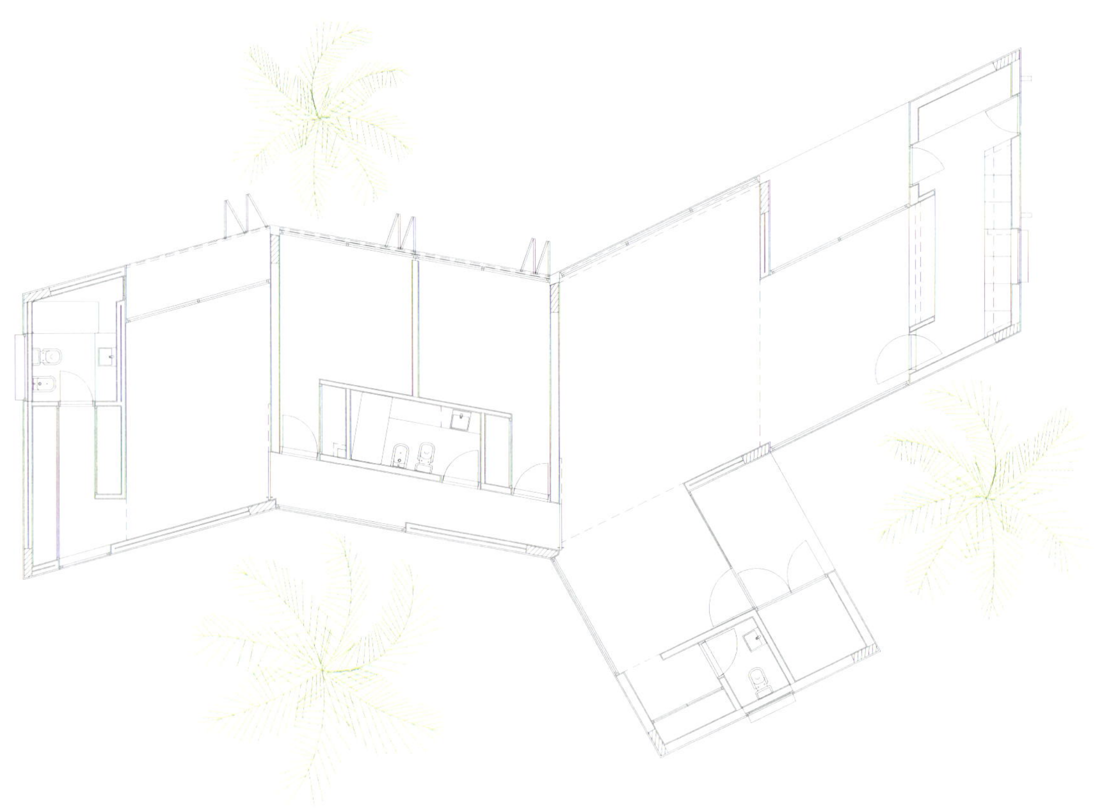

Vignolo house

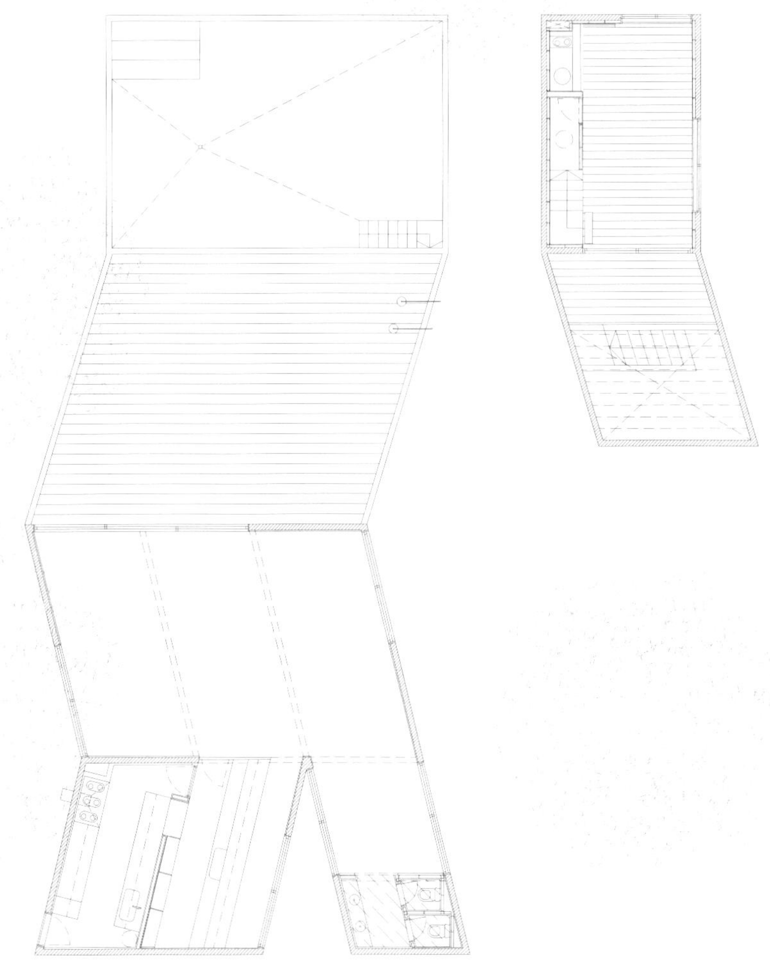

Sociedad de Mar summer residences

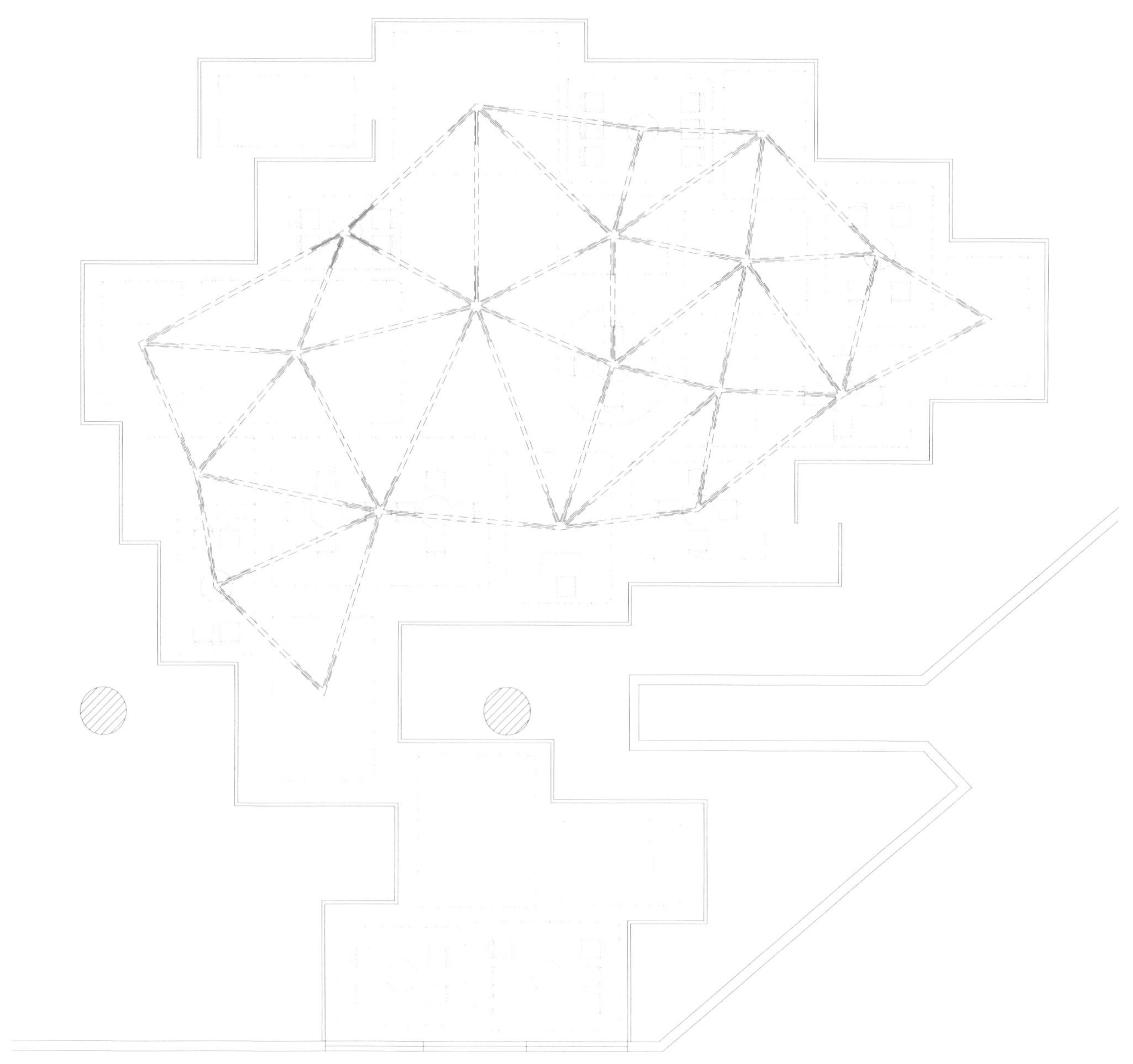

VIP room arteBA

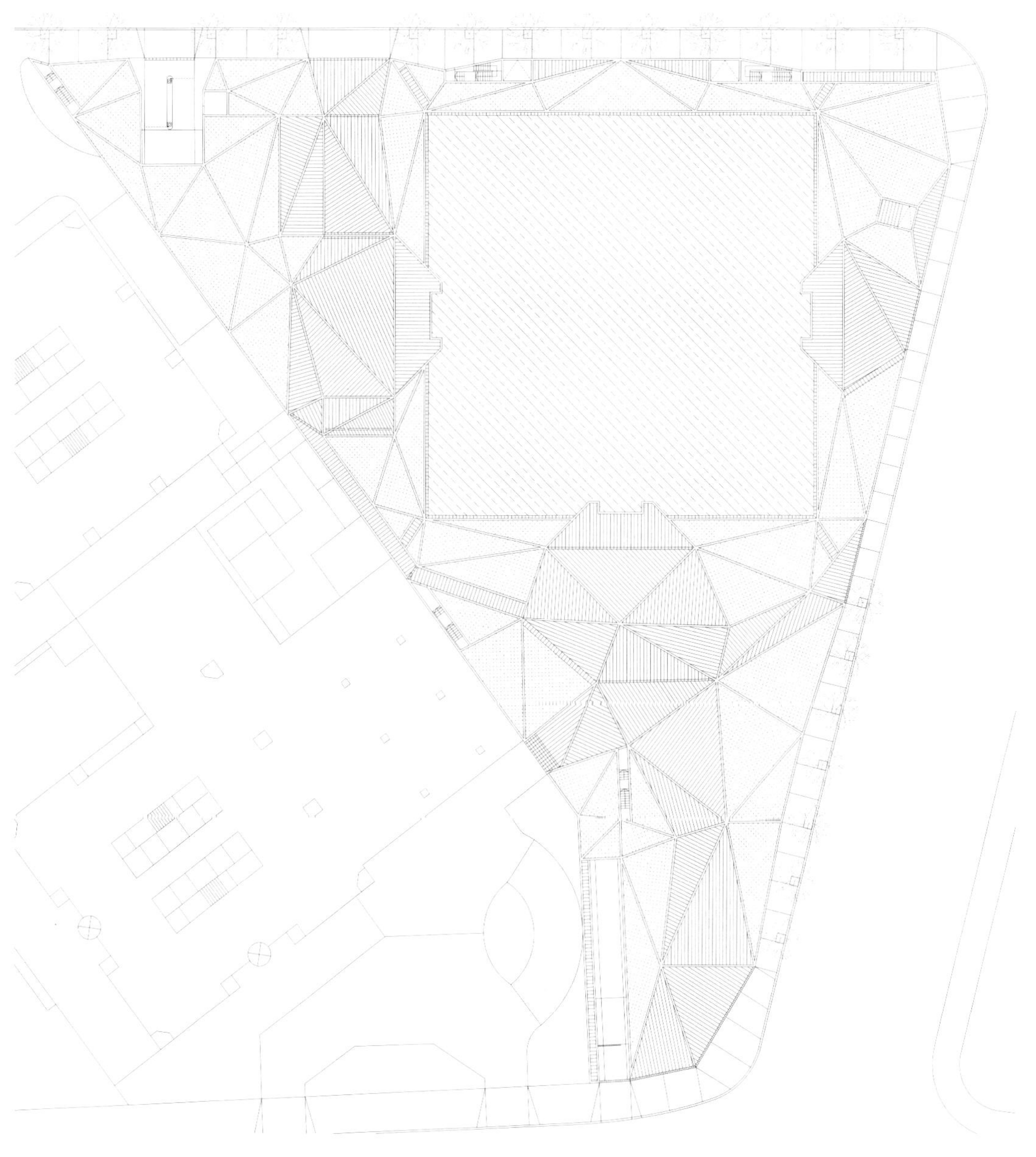

Catalinas square

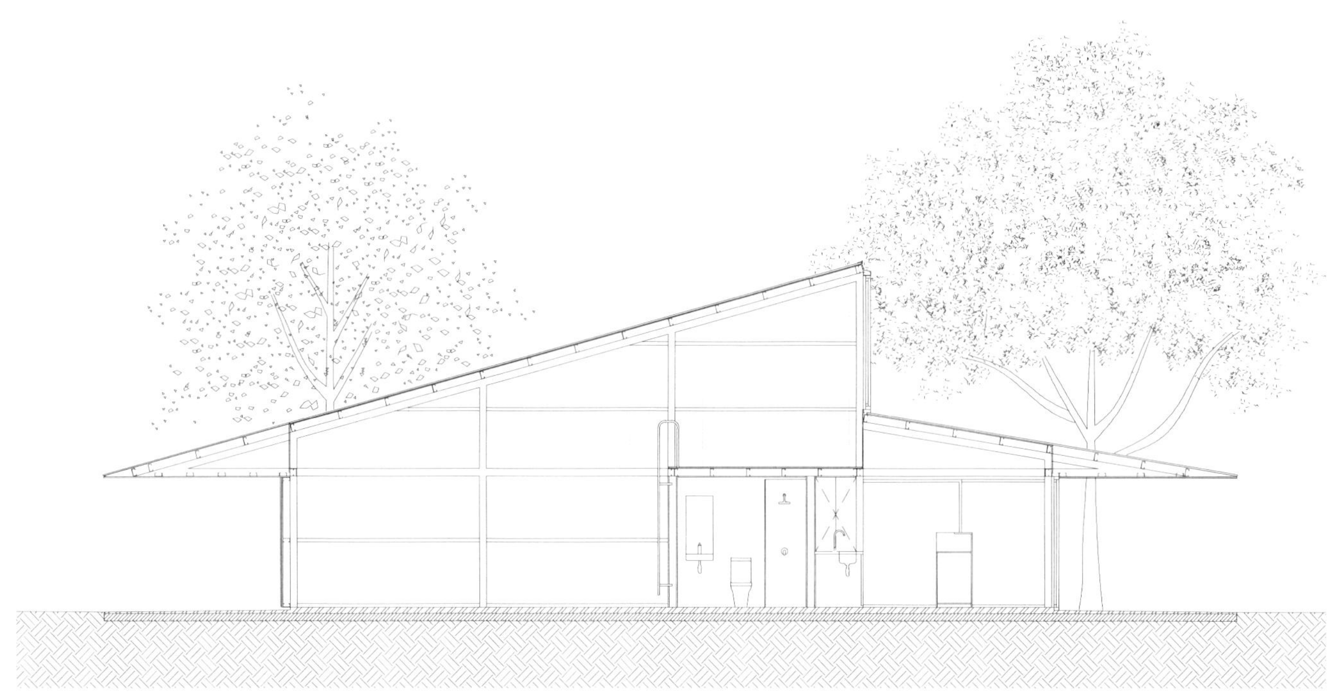

La Juanita's shed

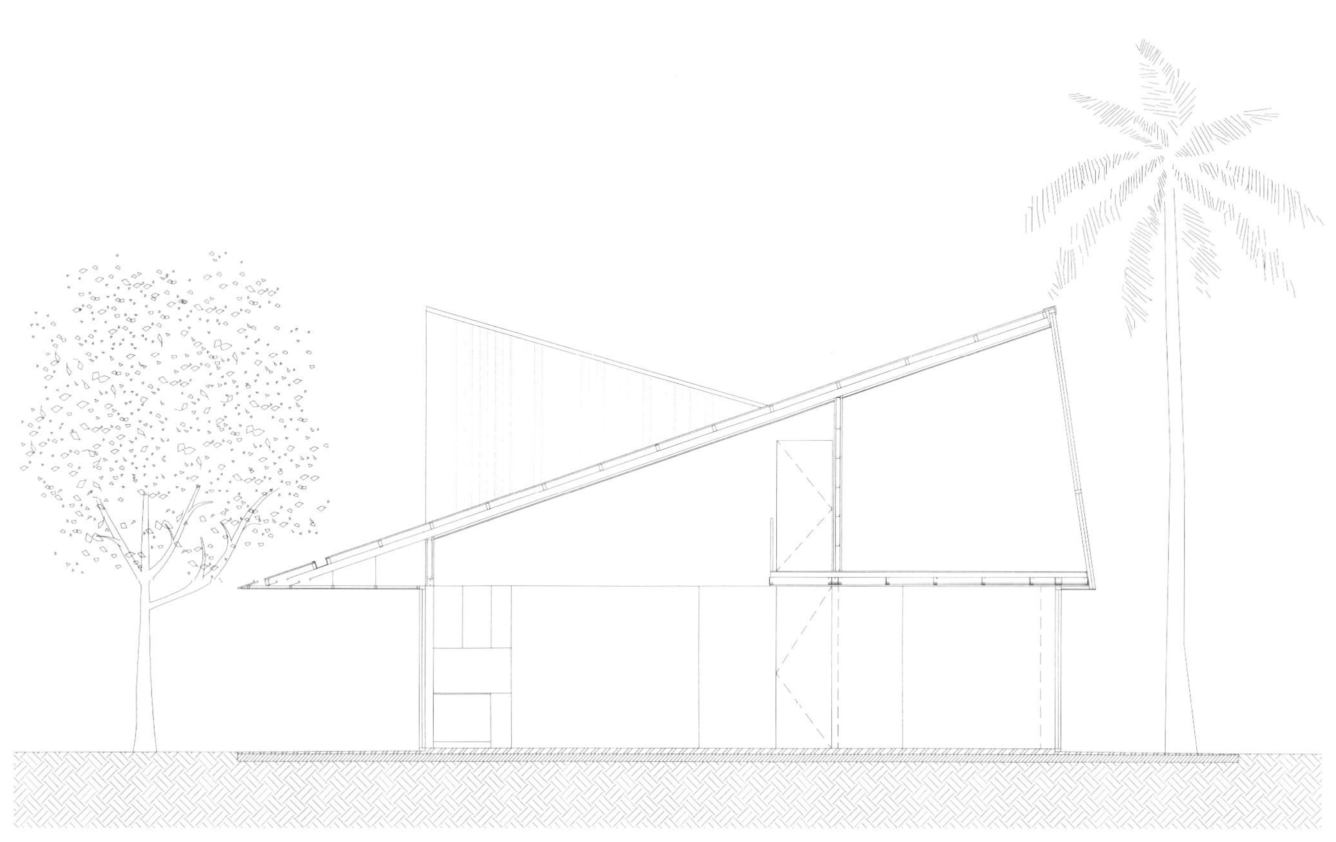

Fukka house

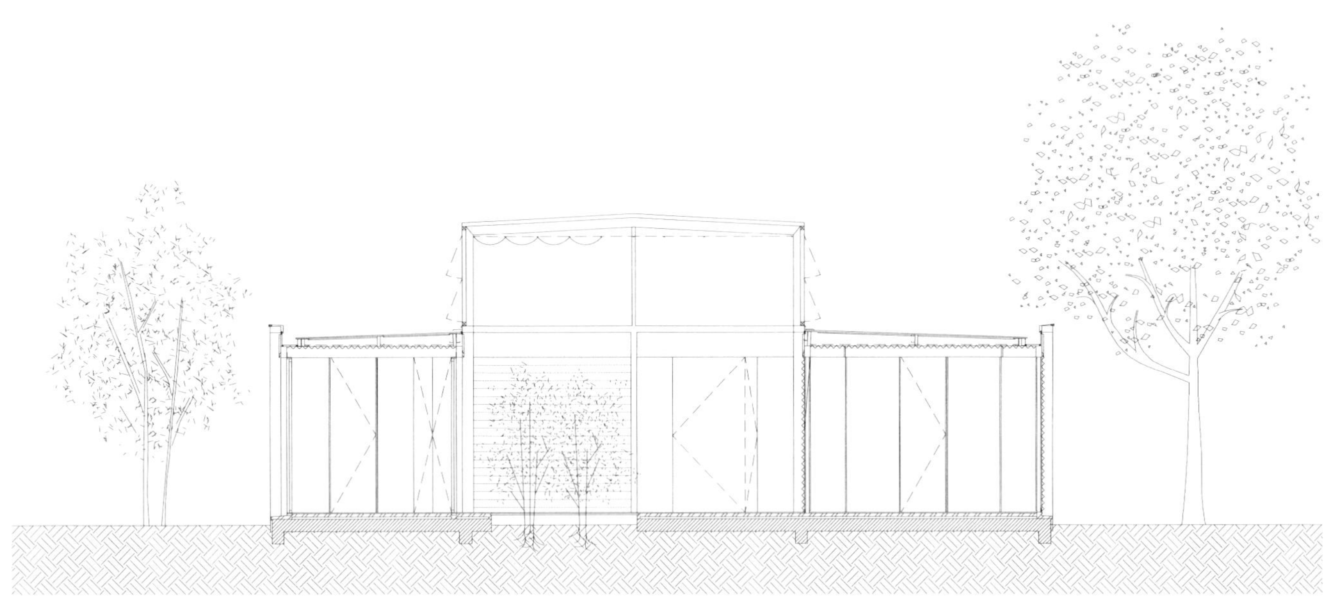

Cepé house

Guayaquil 650 veterinary clinic

Di Tella University pavilion

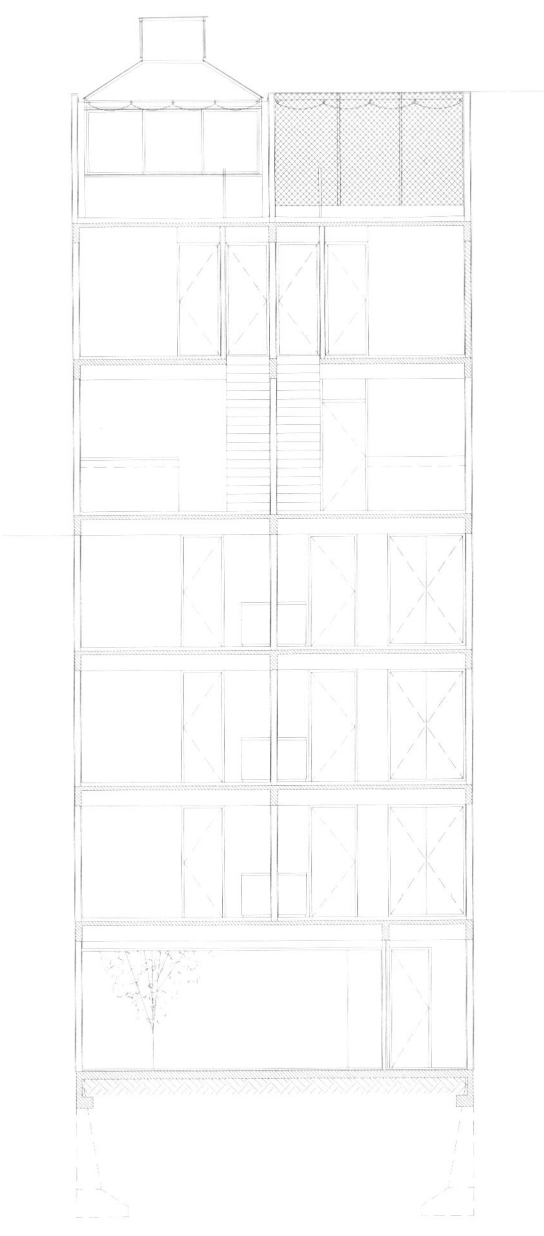

33 Orientales 138 extension

Orno pizzeria

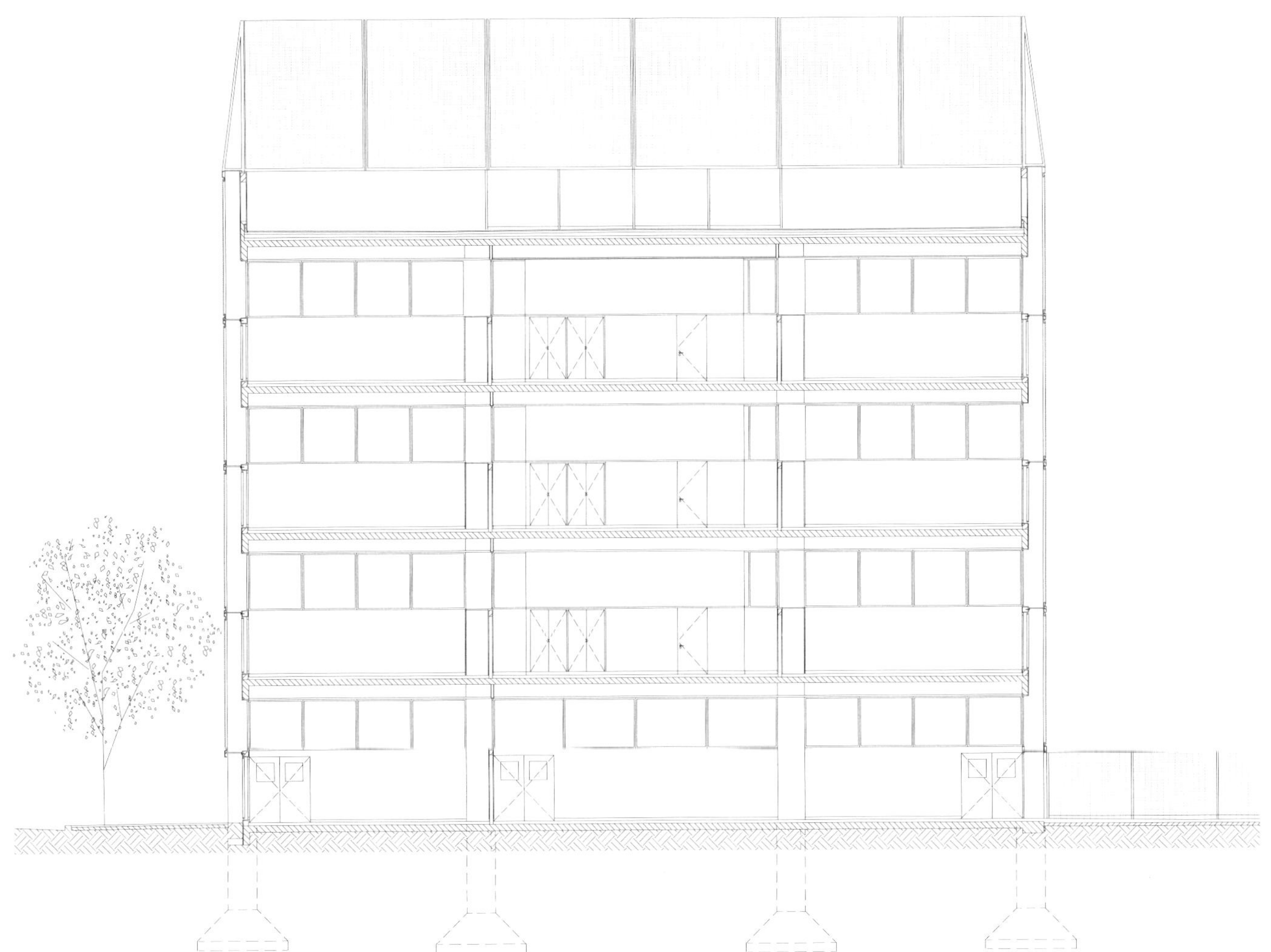

Learning Center plan for Buenos Aires

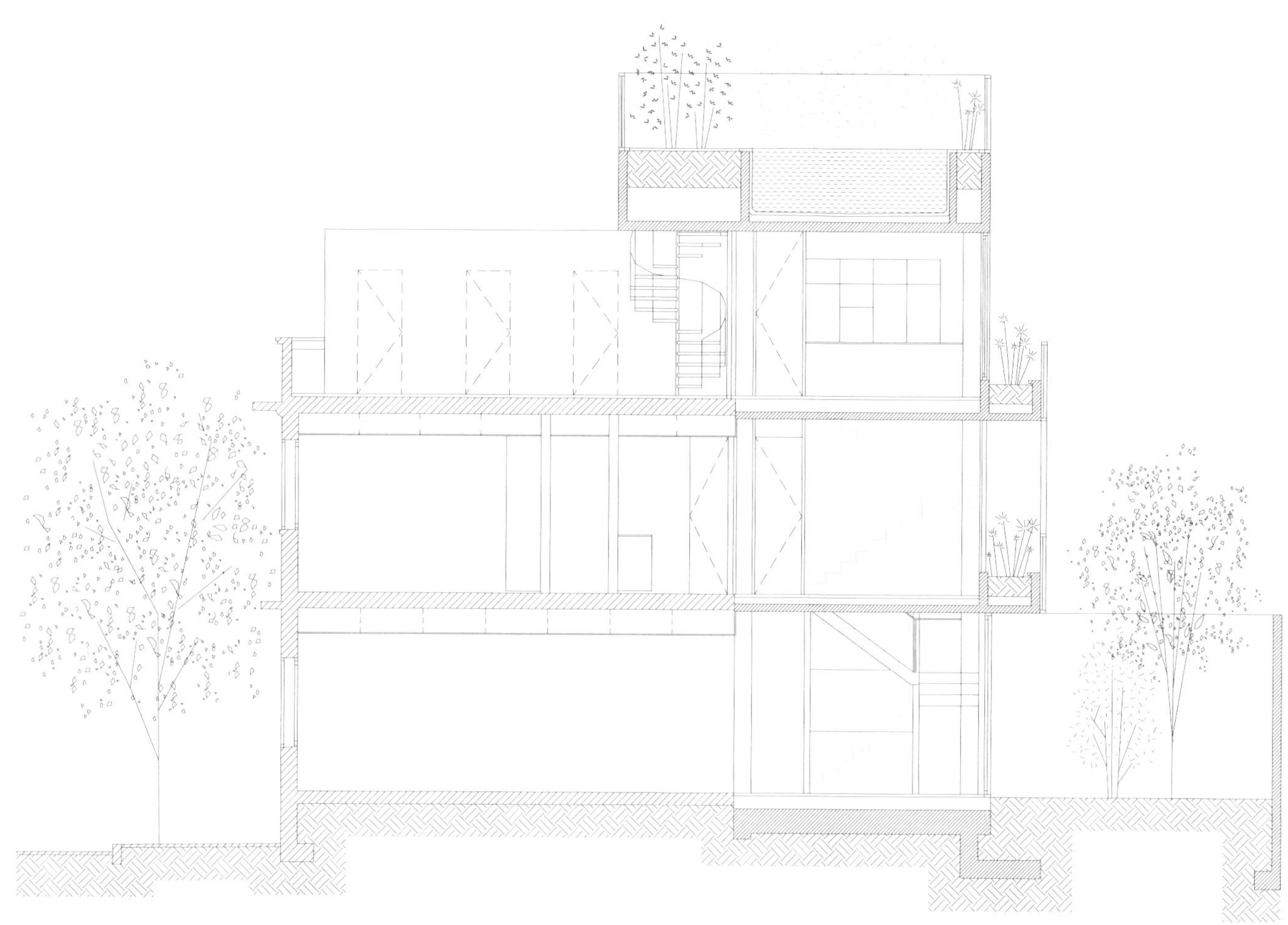

Bedaberes house extension

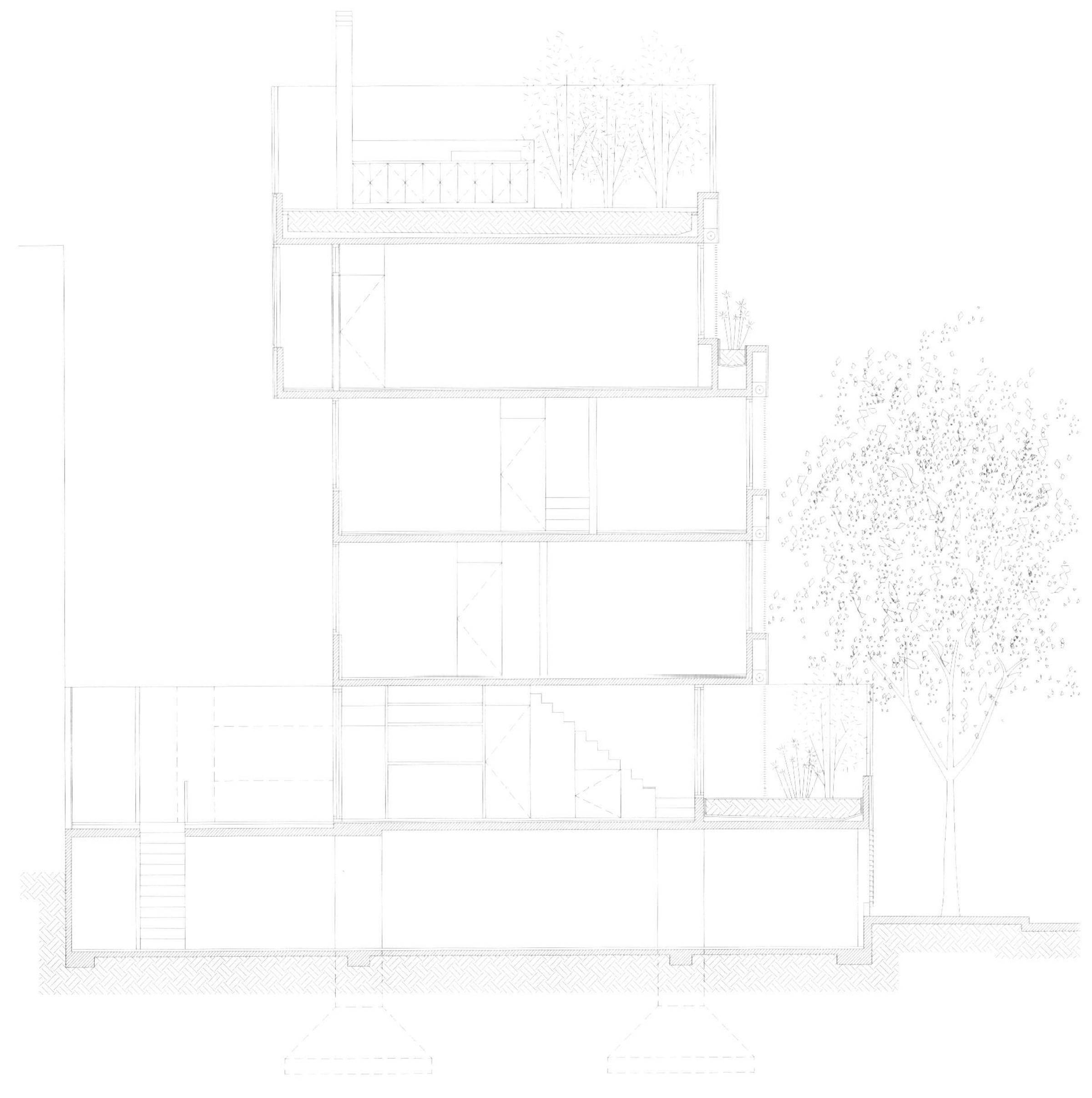

La vecindad Plaza Mafalda building

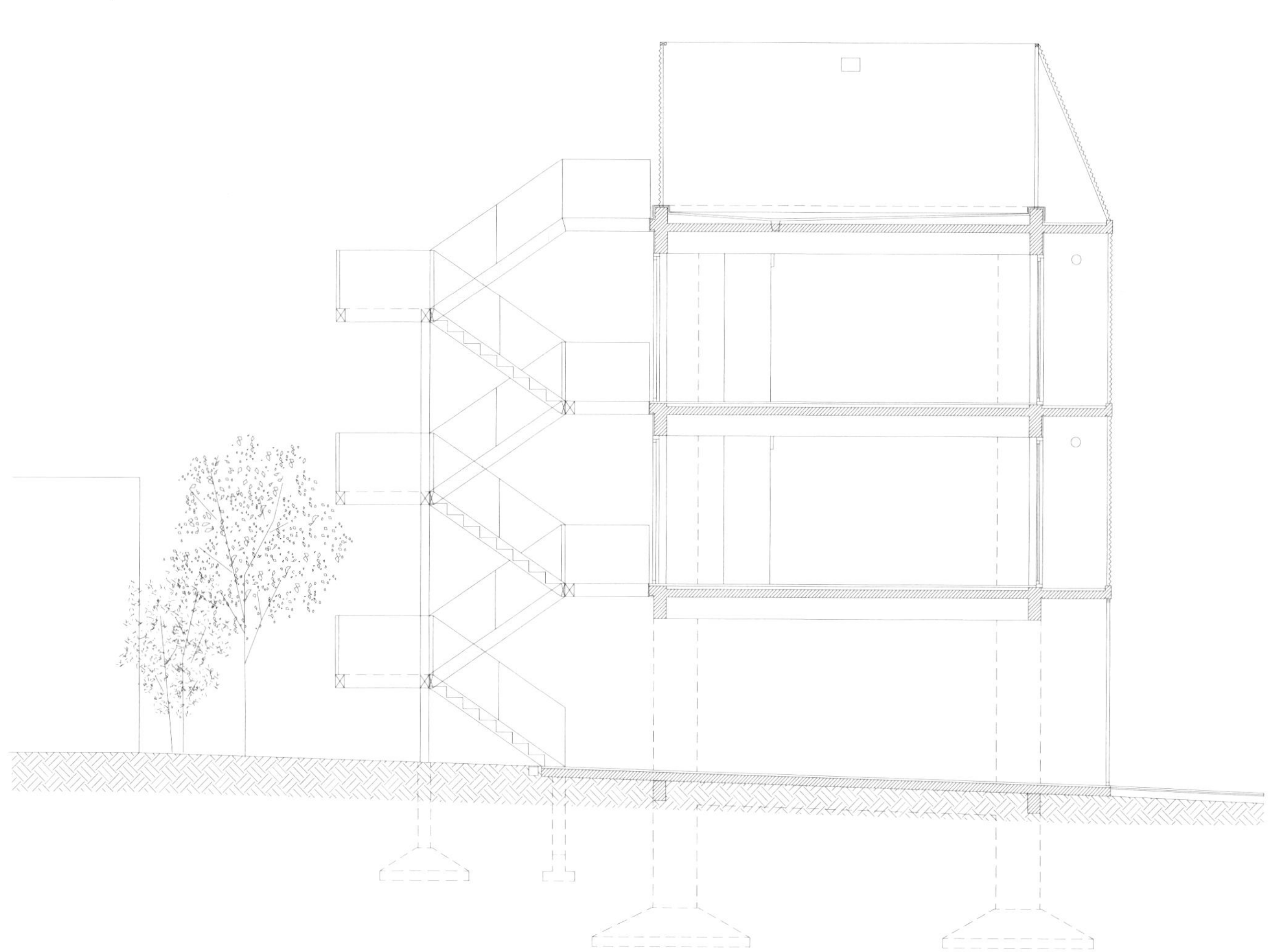

Lago houses

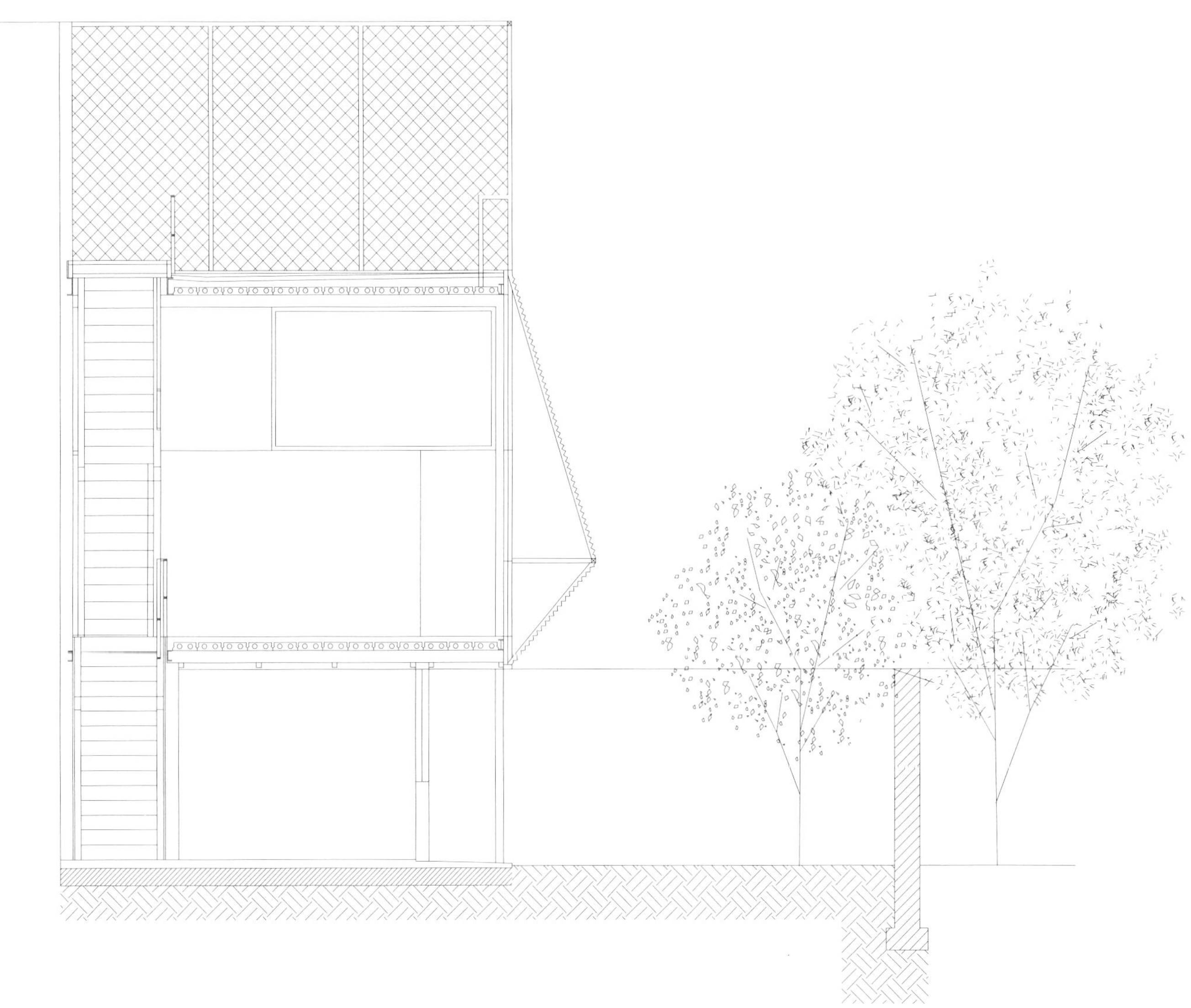

Martos house

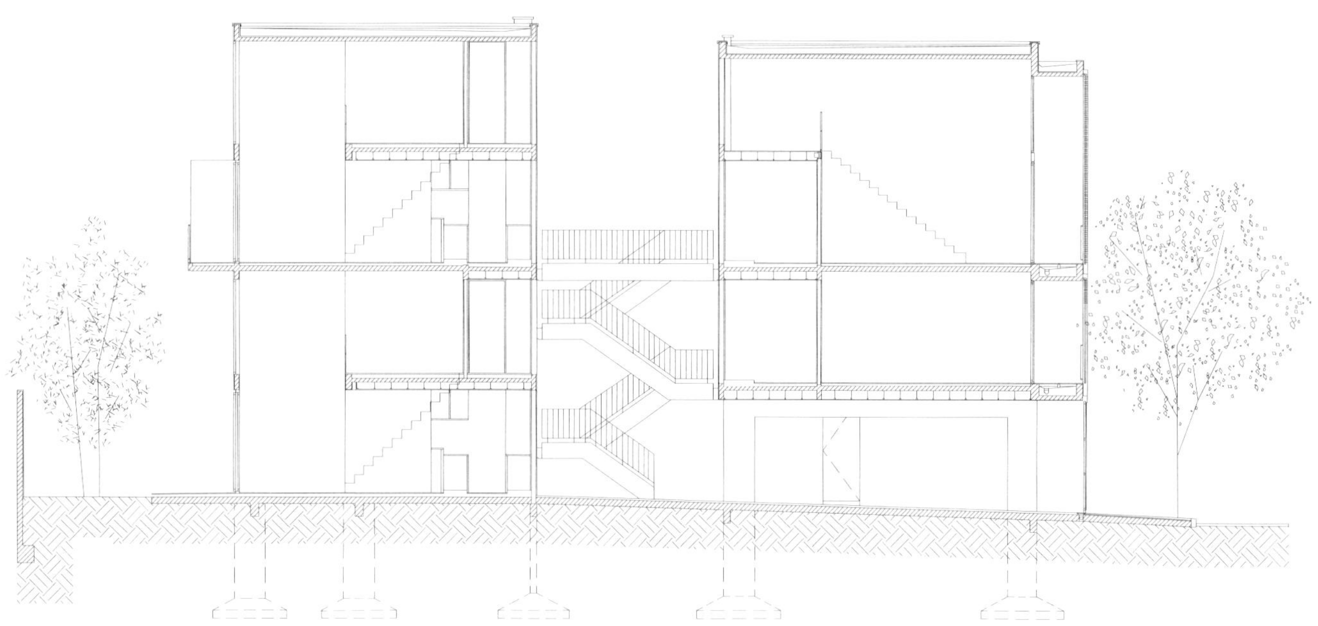

Arribeños 3182 building

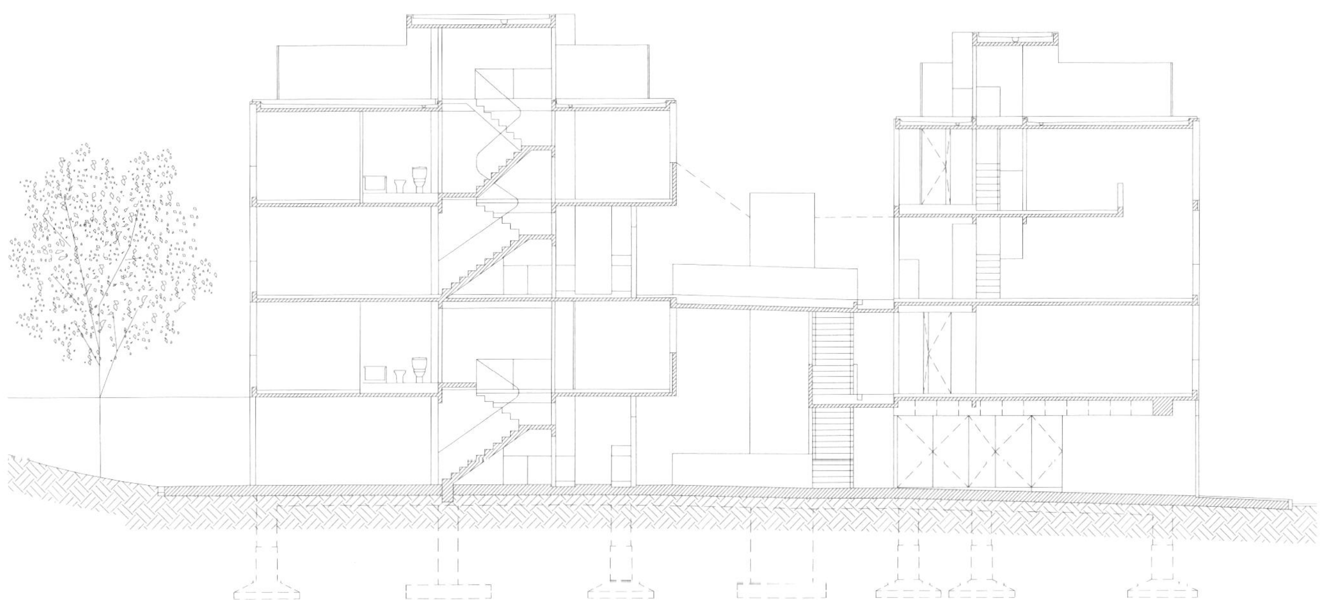

Conesa 4560 building

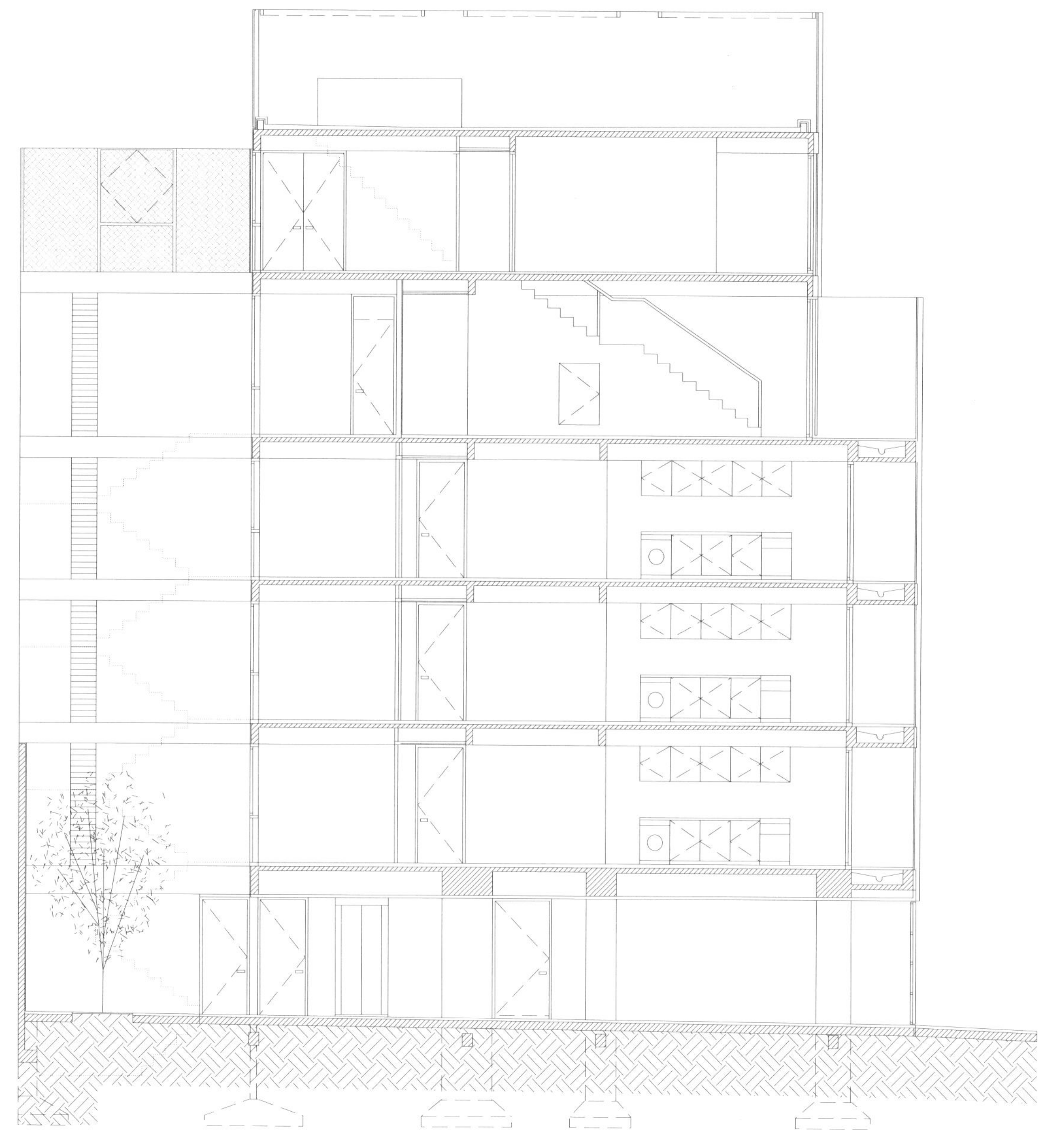

33 Orientales 138 building

Bonpland 2169 building

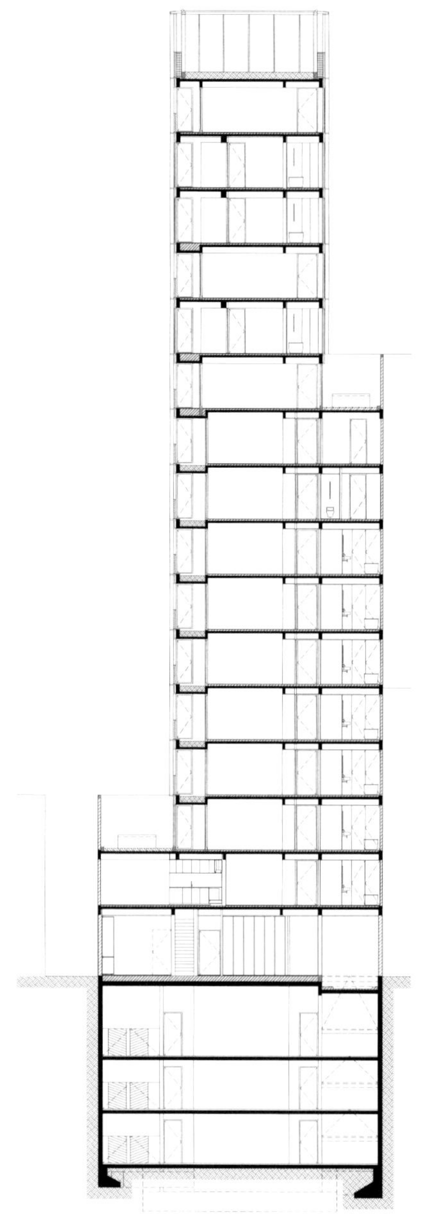

O’Higgins 1625 building

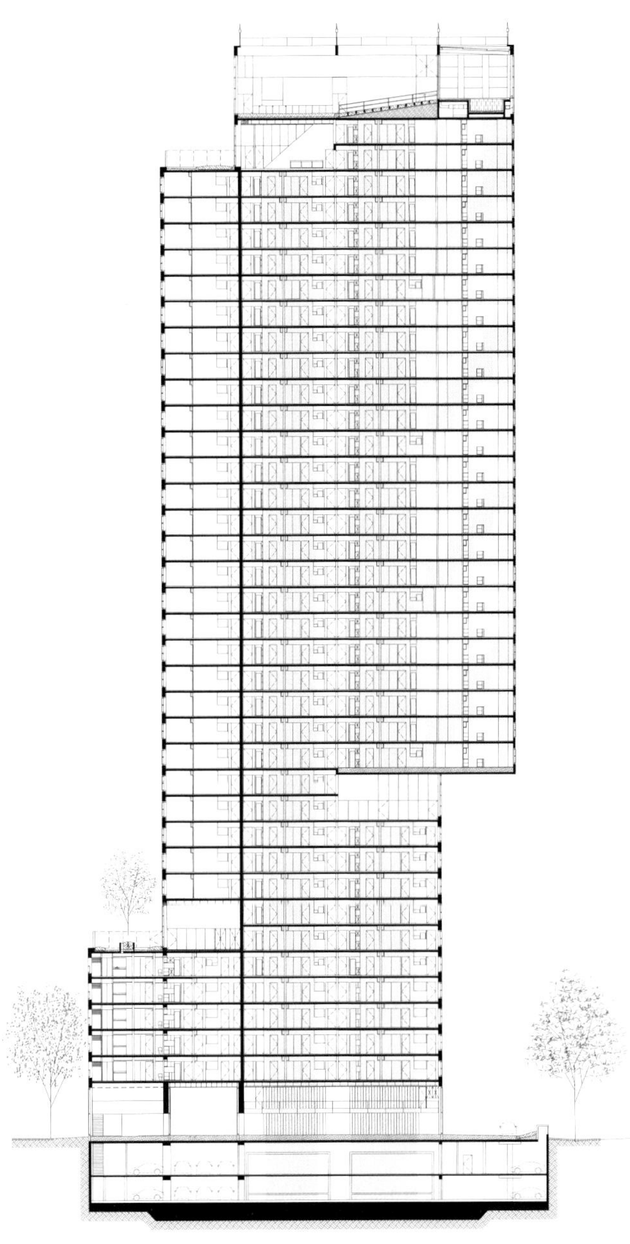

Huergo 475 tower

A Way of Being an Architect

There is a way of being an architect that feeds on desires and demands, overlapping interests and a extensive variety of impulses projected onto architecture from environments that are significantly distant from one another. The design methods and techniques developed by this kind of professional find their maximum potential when facing ordinary situations. The production becomes relevant when no one requests it, almost always and just about anywhere. This way of being an architect is thus associated with a large field of action, an extensive, ductile environment in which to deploy its agenda.

For better or for worse, the city of Buenos Aires favored the development of this way of being an architect. A historically sparse program of competitions prevented the proliferation of architects focusing on public work. The exceptional materializations produced under this system of contracting have become just that: exceptions. Neither the city nor professional practices have been shaped by protected opportunities for projects: that is, for buildings that are desired and produced independently of private interests.

Given this rather unstimulating description, it is worth noting that this same city enjoys a fluid cultural exchange with the world. Ideas have travelled back and forth, through the skies, across the oceans, carried by architects with a universal vocation, eager to participate in the debates taking place in the discipline. It's possible that the architectural production of Buenos Aires has resulted, to a large extent, from the scarcity of institutions that promote it and an extreme desire to practice at any cost. The ones committed to this approach realized that the characteristics of their environment would prevent them from accurately reproducing external models. And instead of offering resistance, they used their entire arsenal of contingencies to unleash a fresh iteration of the same design protocols, making it possible for a context dictated by the laws of the market to offer surprising versions of a disciplinary agenda developed under very different circumstances. This group of architects will be responsible for expanding the elements involved in the project. For them, designing will also imply finding the right position within each economic cycle; it will entail the careful construction of a new kind of client and, above all else, it will require a keen sense of opportunity.

But to describe this way of being an architect more precisely, we may need to go a little deeper. If so far we have referred to the ability to combine an architectural agenda with a context that is challenging, to say the least, now we enter the sphere of private obsessions and fantasies, placed at the service of one's own idea of domesticity. The social and economic conditions of Buenos Aires were accompanied by a dense, compact fabric, built on relatively small plots that were easy to regenerate. This environment gave rise to a fertile territory for testing out new models of collective housing. This will be the chosen typology. The group of architects that will now occupy our attention decided to build their own homes surrounded by other people and other buildings. Dissolved in the landscape of a city that now weaves together a century of history through these buildings. Each case becomes an observatory to rediscover our territory. A place to rise above the ground to gain distant views capable of running through time, renewing the meaning of our ambitions.

This group of architects will not need to build their homes in isolation from the world, enveloped in a stimulating natural landscape, to conceive a work with its own agenda. Nothing could be further from the *carte blanche* represented by the series of houses built and inhabited by the architects that almost all of us know. Here we are interested in those buildings where the real-estate market has imposed its conditions and design has succeeded in overcoming its conventions and evaluation criteria. This way of being an architect goes beyond the traditional scope of the project. It manages a larger volume of variables and handles many more responsibilities, enjoying an enviable freedom of action. The use, the location and the architectural resolution (the what, the where and the how) will become simultaneous design elements of the same hierarchy. Contrary to the increasing incorporation of new specializations in the field of construction, the architects of Buenos Aires will adopt an active resistance set on breaking down the path leading from the project to its future inhabitants. In this way, they will offer a model for building a practice capable of dissolving private obsessions with public needs. And not because a handful of the enlightened practitioners managed to cut this Gordian knot, but because this pragmatic attitude will be transferred from generation to generation, showing how each moment will require a deployment of creativity that will progressively outline a specific model of practice with a profile that is both recognizable and relevant.

33 Orientales 138 building

33 Orientales 138 building

La vecindad Plaza Mafalda building

La vecindad Plaza Mafalda building

Lago houses

Lago houses

Martos house

Martos house

11 de Septiembre 3260 building

11 de Septiembre 3260 building

Núñez house extension

Núñez house extension

Cepé house

Cepé house

Guayaquil 650 veterinary clinic

Guayaquil 650 veterinary clinic

Puertos mixed-use complex

Puertos mixed-use complex

Blas house extension

Blas house extension

Adamo-Faiden
Vão

Luna chair

Luna chair

Airpolis

Triombo

Triombo

Catalinas trash bin

Catalinas square

Salgado house extension

Salgado house extension

La Juanita's shed

La Juanita's shed

Bonpland 2169 building

Bonpland 2169 building

Bedaberes house extension

Bedaberes house extension

33 Orientales 138 extension

33 Orientales 138 extension

The Contemporary Constructor

The contemporary constructor walks down the corridor of a hotel. Countless rooms open onto it. In one, a person can be found writing a book with an atheist theme; in the following, someone is on his knees begging for faith and strength; in a third, a chemist is investigating a form's properties; in a fourth, someone envisions an idealistic metaphysics; and in a fifth, someone else is demonstrating the impossibility of metaphysics. All the rooms share the same corridor. The contemporary constructor must pass through it if he wishes to have a feasible way of entering his own room.

The contemporary constructor understands the world as a collection of concrete facts in perpetual motion, not a puzzle whose pieces will rebuild a whole when pieced together. He describes it as a mosaic without adhesive, with free, multiple loose pieces that are valuable both independently and in related to one another, forming different shifting associations and connections.

The contemporary constructor abandons certainty and objectivity as the goals of thought; he sets himself inside a heterogeneous and unstable context and does so with a certain optimism, understanding that instability and heterogeneity aren't cumbersome accidents, but beautiful creative materials, the genuine object of contemporary imagination.

The contemporary constructor dedicates most of his time to connecting his private ambitions with public needs.

The contemporary constructor lives the city, what is commonplace for those who only have a few things in common.

The contemporary constructor continually broadens his social network. He knows that if he meets only locals, he will stay stuck with the lexicon with which he was educated. Therefore, he tries to acquire the knowledge of other constructors, techniques and unknown surroundings.

The contemporary constructor uses his need to produce as a perfect excuse to study. A studio is a place to study.

The contemporary constructor always converses with history. Without memory, his innovations become mere novelty. History gives his growth direction. But because his memory is never perfect, each memory is an image composed of or degraded from a previous situation or moment. This way, each memory always becomes a new one, a partial construction different from its origin, and, as such, with the potential for self-growth.

The contemporary constructor knows that almost every object can someday become important; he understands the advantage of possessing a general reserve of extra truths or ideas that would be real in possible situations. The contemporary constructor stores those extra truths in his memory and fills his consultation books with the surplus. When one of those extra truths becomes pragmatically relevant for some of his emergencies, it comes out of its cold storage to act in the world, and his belief in it is activated.

The contemporary constructor has a way of thinking that is not a denial of other conceptions; he intersects them, adopts them to generate a particular conversation, igniting new lexicons the validity of which rests not in truth but in verisimilitude, in the ability to create the effect of truth in others through experience.

The contemporary constructor fabricates new words and constantly expands his lexicon. He maintains that new circumstances require a new way of thinking, which in turn requires new forms of expression. His way of expressing himself generates new circumstances.

The contemporary constructor has the ability to formulate his ideas without the need to impose any one in particular; his arguments should be as ignorable as they are interesting.

The contemporary constructor stands on the shoulders of others. He reaches farther piggybacked on the triumphs of those preceding him, and the view is much better.

The contemporary constructor often imitates. He comes as close to the original as he can because he knows that he'll never reach it entirely, and that the difference would be evident. He reminds us how underestimated, discredited and fructiferous imitation is as a technique.

The contemporary constructor maintains a parasitic relationship with his precursors. But because he is conscious of the fact that he will only be able to bring to light a small part of himself, he confides in the benevolence of all those strangers that will find him in the future.

The contemporary constructor converts theories into tools for support, not responses to enigmas. He doesn't lean on them, he moves forward, and on some occasions, reconstructs nature with their help. The contemporary constructor makes all of our theories more flexible, loosens them and puts each of them to work.

Project Credits

Deseos: Installation for the Argentine Pavilion, Venice Biennale. 2006-2006, Buenos Aires, Argentina. Collaborators: Carolina Leveroni, Julián Mastroleo. Client: Argentine Chancellery.

Lago houses. 2005-20 07, Buenos Aires, Argentina. Collaborators: Carolina Leveroni, Luciano Intile, Paula Müller, Luciana Baiocco.

Arribeños 3182 building. 2005-2007, Buenos Aires, Argentina. Collaborators: Carolina Leveroni, Luciano Intile.

Conesa 4560 building. 2006-2008, Buenos Aires, Argentina. Collaborators: Luciano Intile, Aldana Rizza, Gastón Duarte.

Chalú house extension. 2007, Buenos Aires, Argentina. Collaborators: Julián Mastroleo, Paula Müller, Luciana Baiocco.

Vignolo house. 2007-2008, Benavidez, Buenos Aires Province, Argentina. Collaborators: Carolina Leveroni, Luciano Intile, Paula Müller.

La Cándida club house. 2007-2008, La Plata, Buenos Aires Province, Argentina. Collaborators: Luciano Intile, Julián Mastroleo, Flavia Triulzi.

La Cándida community center. 2009, La Plata, Buenos Aires Province, Argentina. Collaborators: Luciano Intile, Hans Rinshofer, Federique Paillard, Juliana Nieva.

Núñez house extension. 2009, Buenos Aires, Argentina. Collaborators: Giuliana Nieva, Iván Fierro, Julien Hosansky, Marie Taillafer de Laportaliere, Carolina Molinari.

MuReRe houses. 2009, Buenos Aires Province, Argentina. Collaborators: Luis Hevia, Carolina Molinari, Arnau Andrés, Ainoha Mugetti, Juliana de Lojo, Natalia Castillo, Juliana Olarte, Ana Kreiman.

The contemporary constructor. Written by Sebastián Adamo and Marcelo Faiden. Published in *Adamo-Faiden*, ARQ serie obras, 2009, Chile; and “Adamo Faiden: El Constructor Contemporáneo”, *TC*, 2018, Spain.

11 de Septiembre 3260 building. 2009-2011, Buenos Aires, Argentina. Collaborators: Luciano Intile, Iván Fierro, Giuliana Nieva, Carolina Molinari, Juliana de Lojo.

Martos house. 2009-2012, Villa Adelina. Buenos Aires Province, Argentina. Collaborators: Ruth Lastra, Virginia Billoch, Rachael Yu.

MuReRe project. Written by Sebastián Adamo and Marcelo Faiden. Published as: “MuReRe houses”, 2009, Argentina.; “MuReRe studio”, Universidad Nacional de La Matanza, 2020, Argentina; “MuReRe project”, 2023, Universidad Torcuato Di Tella, Argentina.

33 Orientales 138 building. 2010-2012, Buenos Aires, Argentina. Collaborators: Ainoha Mugetti, Pablo Garcete, Gonzalo Yerba.

Venturini house extension. 2011, Buenos Aires, Argentina. Collaborators: José Castro Caldas, Flore Silly, Gabriela Schaer.

Sáenz house. 2011-2012. La Plata, Buenos Aires Province, Argentina. Collaborators: Juliana de Lojo, Gonzalo Yerba.

Hydro Industrial pavillion. 2011-2012, Pilar, Buenos Aires Province, Argentina. Associate: Daniel Silberfaden. Collaborator: Gonzalo Yerba.

Sociedad de Mar summer residences. 2011-2014, José Ignacio, Maldonado Department, Uruguay. Collaborators: Gonzalo Yerba, Javier Bracamonte, Nicolás Frenkiel, Florencia Tortorelli, Julia Hajnal.

Catalinas square. 2011-2017, Buenos Aires, Argentina. Collaborators: Nicolás Frenkiel, Javier Bracamonte, Luis Hevia, Gonzalo Yerba, Noelia García Lofredo, Florencia Tortorelli, María Alejandra González, Martín Zlobec, Andrea Carnero, Damiano Finetti, Julia Hajnal, Cynthia Szwarcberg, Simona Solorzano, Judith Käding, Santiago Giusto. Client: Consultatio S.A.

Catalinas trash bin. 2011-2017, Buenos Aires, Argentina. Producer: Ries. Client: Consultatio S.A.

Triombo: Installation for Monoambiente Gallery. 2013, Buenos Aires, Argentina. Curator: Martín Huberman. Producer: La Feliz.

The work of others. Written by Sebastián Adamo and Marcelo Faiden. Published in: *2G* no. 65 “Adamo-Faiden”, Gustavo Gili, 2013, Spain.

Blas house extension. 2014-2015, Buenos Aires, Argentina. Collaborators: Jaime Butler, Paula Araujo, María Ribes Eritja.

Fernández house extension. 2014-2015, Buenos Aires, Argentina. Collaborators: Jaime Butler, Gonzalo Yerba, Paula Araujo Varas.

Piñeiro house extension. 2015, Buenos Aires, Argentina. Collaborators: Damiano Finetti.

Eco tourism tower. 2015, Las Perlas, Panamá. Collaborators: Marcos Altgelt, Martina De Barba, Adrián Trujillo.

VIP room arteBA. 2016, Buenos Aires, Argentina. Collaborators: Juan Campanini.

Macchi house extension. 2016-2018, Lobos, Buenos Aires Province, Argentina. Collaborators: Javier Gómez, Esteban Lamm, Darío Graschinsky.

Bonpland 2169 building. 2016-2018, Buenos Aires, Argentina. Collaborators: Paula Araujo Varas, Ezequiel Estepo, Marcos Altgelt, Martina De Barba

La vecindad Plaza Mafalda building. 2016-2018, Buenos Aires, Argentina. Collaborators: Javier Gómez, Sofía Harsich, Esteban Lamm, Julia Chiozza, Pedro Magnasco. Client: Compañía de Inversión y Desarrollo.

Puertos mixed-use complex. 2016-2022, Escobar, Buenos Aires Province, Argentina. Collaborators: Priscila Ra, Ana Isaía, Victoria Irigoyen, Derrick Christensen, Lucas Bruno, Enzo Fabriccio De Dio, Tomas Guerrini, Luciana Lembo, Juan Campanini, Iñaki Harosteguy, Gianfranco Francioni, Lucía Padilla, Juan Tohme, Felipe Buigues, Marcos Altgelt. Client: Consultatio S.A.

Learning Center plan for Buenos Aires. 2017, Buenos Aires, Argentina. Project Directors: Sebastián Adamo, Marcelo Faiden, Mariano Clusellas. General Director of Urban Innovation of the Ministry of Urban Development and Transport: Martín Torrado (Torrado Arquitectos). Team: Gonzalo Yerba, Javier Bracamonte (BHY arquitectos), Javier Esteban (Esteban-Tannenbaum), Ainoha Mugetti, Juliana de Lojo (MDLarqs), Mariano Pensado. Cynthia Szwarcberg, Leonardo Valdivieso, Connie Odell, Julieta da Costa, Marina Alejandra Balduzzi, Maximiliano Rostan, Lucia Ayerbe Rant. Client: Gobierno de la Ciudad de Buenos Aires.

Luar house extension. 2018-2019, Vicente López. Buenos Aires Province, Argentina. Collaborators: Jonathan Lee, Paula Araujo Varas.

Cepé house. 2018-2021, Hudson, Buenos Aires Province, Argentina. Collaborators: Jeronimo Bailat, Sofía Harsich, Manuel Marcos.

Puertos sport club. 2018-2023, Escobar, Buenos Aires Province, Argentina. Collaborators: Priscila Ra, Ana Isaía, Victoria Irigoyen, Derrick Christensen, Tomás Guerrini, Lucas Bruno, Iñaki Harosteguy, Gianfranco Francioni, Luciana Lembo, Darío Graschinsky. Client: Consultatio S.A.

Huergo 475 tower. 2018-2024, Buenos Aires, Argentina. Collaborators: Luciana Lembo (Project Director), Mora Linares, Priscila Ra, Enzo Fabriccio De Dio, Ana Isaía, Clara Fragueiro, Rocío Monje, Germán Ferradas, Seizen Uehara, Jonathan Lee, Sofía Harsich, Manuel Marcos, Tomás Guerrini, Jerónimo Bailat, Agustín Fiorito, Tomás Pérez Amenta, Dylan Lis, Birk Satuber, Tomás Bueri, Horacio Fridman, Sebastián Comito, César Paganelli, Francisco Remón, Matías Muxi, Agustín Calvetti, Renzo Scotto d'Abusco. Client: Consultatio S.A.

33 Orientales 138 extension. 2019, Buenos Aires, Argentina. Collaborators: Paula Araujo Varas.

Gianelli mixed-use complex. 2019-2019. Montevideo, Uruguay. Associates: Agustín Fiorito, Massimiliano Fraga, Diego Baglini. Collaborators: Luciana Lembo, Tomás Guerrini, Tomás Pérez Amenta, Jerónimo Bailat, Manuel Marcos.

O que vemos, o que nos olha: Installation for the São Paulo Biennale. 2019, São Paulo, Brasil. Associates: Vão arquitetura (Anna Juni, Enk te Winkel, Gustavo Delonero).

Airpolis: Installation for Quick Tiny Shows / MALBA Museum. 2019, Buenos Aires, Argentina. Collaborators: Paula Araujo Varas, Sofía Harsich, Agustín Fiorito.

A way of being an architect. Based on the design seminar: "My House, My City". 2019, Princeton SoA. Published online at the Canadian Centre for Architecture, 2021.

Bedaberes house extension. 2019-2021, Buenos Aires, Argentina. Collaborators: Lucas Bruno (Project Director), Sofía Araujo Varas, Derrick Christensen.

Oro 1778 parking. 2019-2023, Buenos Aires, Argentina. Collaborators: Jonathan Lee (Project Director), Luciana Charroqui, Lucas Bruno, Cesar Paganelli, Horacio Fridman, Natalia Medrano, Sofía Carena, Agustín Fiorito, Federico Knichnik, Agustín Calvetti.

Ático Boulevard Labrador building. 2019-2024, Buenos Aires, Argentina. Collaborators: Sofía Harsich (Project Director), Julieta Zizmond, Rocío Monje, Diego Constanzo, Sofía Svaton, Paula Pockay, Renzo Scotto d'Abusco, Federico Knichnik, Lucas Beizo. Client: Compañía de Inversión y Desarrollo.

Salgado house extension. 2020, La Paloma, Rocha Department , Uruguay. Associate: Agustín Fiorito. Collaborators: Manuel Marcos, Tomás Pérez Amenta.

Optical retail. 2020, Montevideo, Uruguay. Associate: Agustín Fiorito. Collaborators: Manuel Marcos, Lucía Villarreal, Camila Iglesias.

Fukka house. 2020-2022, Garín, Buenos Aires Province, Argentina. Collaborators: Emilia Fernández, Luciana Lembo, Tomás Pérez Amenta.

Bernardello house extension. 2020-2022, Vicente López, Buenos Aires Province, Argentina. Collaborators: Jonathan Lee (Project Director), Natalia Medrano, Sofía Carena, Germán Ferradas.

Guayaquil 650 veterinary clinic. 2020-2022, Buenos Aires, Argentina. Collaborators: Sofía Araujo Varas, Sofía Carena, Jerónimo Bailat.

Gonzalo Ramírez 1441 social housing. 2020-2023, Montevideo, Uruguay. Associate: Agustín Fiorito. Collaborators: Manuel Marcos, Lucía Villarreal, Camila Iglesias. Client: SITU.

Orno pizzeria. 2020-2023, Buenos Aires, Argentina. Associates: Chamber Projects (Juan García Mosqueda). Collaborators: Paula Araujo (Project Director), Sofía Harsich, Tomás Pérez Amenta, Lucas Beizo, Julieta Zizmond, Florencia Stilman, Clara Bellocq, Martina Pera.

A permeable curtain wall. Written by Sebastián Adamo and Marcelo Faiden. Published in *A+U* no. 610 "House Looking Into The World", 2021, Japan.

O'Higgins 1625 building. 2020-2024, Buenos Aires, Argentina. Collaborators: Tomás Pérez Amenta (Project Director), Lucas Beizo, Emilia Fernández, Jerónimo Marquez, Matías Nola, Paula Pockay, Federico Knichnik, Renzo Scotto D'Abusco, Sofía Svaton, Julieta Zizmond.
Client: Chamber Projects.

Figueroa house. 2021, Playa verde, Maldonado Department, Uruguay. Associate: Agustín Fiorito. Collaborators: Manuel Marcos, Lucía Villarreal, Camila Iglesias.

Embassy of the Republic of Philippines extension. 2021, Buenos Aires, Argentina. Collaborators: Paula Araujo (project director), Luciana Charroqui, Manuel Marcos, Tomás Pérez Amenta, Lucas Beizo, Florencia Stilman, Luciana Lembo, Sofia Harsich.

Luna chair: Installation for 8 1/2 gallery. 2021, Montevideo, Uruguay. Associate: Agustín Fiorito. Collaborators: Lucía Villarreal, Camila Iglesias.

Mid-week house. 2021-2023, Luján. Buenos Aires Province, Argentina. Associates: arrhov frick (Johan Arrhov, Henrik Frick). Collaborators: Emilia Fernández, Lucas Beizo.

Núñez house. 2021-2022, Pilar. Buenos Aires Province, Argentina. Collaborators: Clara Fragueiro, Manuel Marcos, Derrick Christensen, Sofía Carena.

La Juanita's shed. 2021-2022, Punta Negra, Departamento de Maldonado, Uruguay. Associate: Agustín Fiorito. Collaborators: Lucía Villarreal, Camila Iglesias, Manuel Marcos.

Andes 1143 social housing. 2021-2024, Montevideo, Uruguay. Associate: Agustín Fiorito. Collaborators: Lucía Villarreal, Camila Iglesias, Manuel Marcos.

Di Tella University pavilion. 2022-2023, Buenos Aires, Argentina. Collaborators: Mora Linares, Manuel Heck, Agustín Calvetti.

Inventory. Written by Sebastián Adamo and Marcelo Faiden, 2022, Buenos Aires.

Photography Credits

adamo-faiden
008, 009, 017, 019, 021, 022, 025, 027, 028, 035, 041, 042, 048, 050, 054, 062, 064, 078, 098, 106, 108, 114, 118, 132, 134, 183, 187, 188,189, 190, 196, 205, 207, 208, 210, 215, 216, 219, 220.

André Scarpa
136, 203

Cristóbal Palma
004, 005, 010, 023, 024, 029, 052, 056, 082, 116, 122, 130, 191, 193, 194.

Ethan De Clerk
012, 043, 044.

Fran Parente
201, 202.

Francisco Berreteaga
003, 007, 033, 080, 120.

Gustavo Sosa Pinilla
124.

Javier Agustín Rojas
006, 011, 013, 014, 015, 018, 020, 026, 030, 031, 032, 034, 036, 037, 038, 039, 040, 058, 060, 066, 068, 070, 072, 074, 084, 086, 088, 090, 092, 094, 096, 100, 102, 104, 110, 112, 128, 185, 186, 192, 195, 197, 198, 199, 200, 204, 206, 209, 211, 212, 213, 214, 217, 218.

María Pía Castro de La Torre
184.

Sergio Pirrone
016, 126.

Acknowledgements

The documents presented in Inventory are the product of the intense work carried out over a period of 18 years, which was developed as a team with an amazing group of people who actively participated in the conversations that gave birth to all our projects. Likewise, through the years we have had the unconditional support of family, friends and clients who were an inseparable part of the work carried out. We would like to express our most affectionate gratitude to all of them.

During the process of putting together this book, we had the privilege of exchanging ideas and points of view with Iñaki Ábalos, Enrique Walker, Florian Idemburg, Florencia Rodríguez, Alexandre Theriot, Uriel Fogué, Felipe de Ferrari, Juan García Mosqueda, Leandro Chiappa, Gustavo Eandi, María Pía Castro de La Torre and Javier Agustín Rojas. To all of them, we are deeply grateful.

Inventory
adamo-faiden

Published by
Actar Publishers
New York / Barcelona
www.actar.com

Authors
adamo-faiden
Sebastián Adamo,
Marcelo Faiden

Editorial Coordination
Franco Brachetta & Sofia Carena (adamo-faiden).
Candela De Bortoli (Actar)

Copy-editing
Angela Bunning

Printing and Binding
Arlequin & Pierrot SL

Printed in Spain

Publication date
March 2023

ISBN: 978-1-63840-035-6
LCCN: 2022942762

A CIP catalogue record for this book is available from the Library of Congress, Washington, DC, USA.

Distributed by
Actar D, Inc.

New York
440 Park Avenue South, 17 Fl.
New York, NY 10016, USA
+12129662207
salesnewyork@actar-d.com

Barcelona
Roca i Batlle, 2-4
08023 Barcelona, Spain
+34 933 282 183
eurosales@actar-d.com